Hey Rich —
Sorry to hear
you're having to battle
The Beast. I lost a
testicle + the vision (to cancer)
in my right eye, so now

DOES THIS BOOK

MAKE MY HEAD LOOK

FAT?

I'm half blind and
half nuts!
Enjoy, and
all the best!

D1512065

DOES THIS BOOK

MAKE MY HEAD LOOK

FAT?

Mack Dryden

Texas Review Press
Huntsville, Texas

FIRST EDITION, 2013
Requests for permission to reproduce material from this work should be
sent to:

    Permissions
    Texas Review Press
    English Department
    Sam Houston State University
    Huntsville, TX 77341-2146

Cover design: Elise Fazio of Fitzio.com

Cover photos: Brian Bohannon

Library of Congress Cataloging-in-Publication Data

Dryden, Mack.
  Does this book make my head look fat? / Mack
Dryden.
    pages cm
  ISBN 978-1-937875-03-9 (pbk. : alk. paper)
  1. American wit and humor. I. Title.
  PN2287.D75A25 2013
  792.702'8092--dc23
                       2012044069

For Teri, my soul mate and best audient,

and Dad, whose greatest gift to me was a sense of humor

CONTENTS

—177—

buster Babcock's

BACHELOR BRIEFS:

a survival guide for single guys

DOES THIS BOOK

MAKE MY HEAD LOOK

FAT?

INTRODUCTION:
MY ONLY SUPER POWER

My fourth grade teacher—I'll call her Mrs. Samuels—was a stern, humorless woman who ran a military-style classroom and put up with zero foolishness. The atmosphere was oppressive for a playful kid like me, because I lived for foolishness, having discovered very early that I had a knack for making people laugh.

A new boy named Johnny joined our class and was seated next to me by alphabetical accident. He was big for his age and shy, and I was small for my age and not. He helped out at his parents' gas station, and at the tender age of 10 was sleep-deprived and always had engine grease under his fingernails. I befriended him because he was friendless and obviously had a difficult home life on the rougher side of the tracks.

Johnny shadowed me at recess because I kept his tickle-box rolling, and I loved practicing my foolishness on him. Plus, he was a very effective bodyguard, with his grown-up swagger and hands as hard as brake pads. Bullies tend to target kids who are smarter, funnier, and of course smaller than they are, so Johnny and I had a comfortable symbiosis.

When Mrs. Samuels would turn her back to

the class to write something on the blackboard, Johnny often took the opportunity to reach across the aisle and plant a folded sheet of paper on my desk. He wasn't quick with the verbal quip, but with the written word he had time to organize a thought before trying to get his comedy mentor to favor him with a chuckle. I usually reacted with a smile and a wink, which satisfied him. One day he sent a note suggesting that Charlene Elmore's angular face and bulging eyes made her look like a billy goat. Below his note I wrote: "That's a terrible thing to say about billy goats," and passed it back at the first opportunity. This caused a respiratory explosion in Johnny that he covered with a coughing fit, and I felt the tingle of power in my pencil.

One day he slipped me his drawing of what was supposed to be the female genitalia— basically a forked twig with a nub in the middle. Using the arms of the Y as eyebrows, I extended the lines and drew a pretty decent caricature of a stern old woman's face, with eyeglasses dangling from her neck on a chain so Johnny would recognize our teacher immediately.

I slipped it back to him, then watched as he unfolded it and unleashed a machinegun burst of giggles before he could engage the safety. Mrs. Samuels spun from the blackboard and fixed him with a death-ray glare. "Something funny, Mr. Fulford?"

He tried to disappear behind the student sitting in front of him as he stuffed the paper down the front of his jeans, where she wouldn't dare search him. "No ma'am," he said. "I just thought of something I saw on TV last night."

She shifted her all-seeing laser stare to me,

which ignited a guilty glow on my face. "You sure it wasn't the Mackie Dryden Show?"

I don't remember if we got paddled for that infraction or not—the memories of my many paddlings blend and blur—but the event was a dramatic demonstration of a skill I had from an early age that eventually became my career. I got thousands of laughs in school, most of them unpunished; but making Johnny laugh at pencil scratching on notebook paper was special: I hadn't made a face, mewled a sound effect, or uttered a word. Johnny didn't *want* to draw attention to himself and incur the wrath of Mrs. Samuels. So, using only black lines on white paper—which are what written words are as well—*and against Johnny's will*, I had *forced* him to laugh when he didn't want to! To me, that approaches a magical power, like waving a wand and making a pro wrestler sing an aria from *Rigoletto*.

If you happened to encounter an alien whose home planet was devoid of humor, you might show him footage of some classic slapstick comedians and the wackier sitcoms and get him to understand why humans laugh at such inspired silliness. But if you tried to make him understand that earthlings also laugh uproariously at black lines and symbols like these arranged on a white page in an inert stack of paper and ink, he might think you were pulling his tripod.

As I got older, my appreciation of the power grew as I read Twain and Wodehouse, Thurber and Vonnegut, and realized they were making me laugh out loud *from the grave*, so this White Magic is both edifying and enduring. I set out to learn its secrets, and there's nothing that makes my heart soar like knowing I've caused someone somewhere to horselaugh or—even better—to stifle a laugh and blow a beverage through his nose because he doesn't want people to think he's nuts for laughing alone.

I wouldn't wish you nasal discomfort; but if you read this in public, I do hope you draw unwanted attention to yourself with a cackle. Forgive me, but it's what I live for.

POTTING THE ANTEBELLUM CONTAGIOUS

I confess I was mildly disturbed when my wife told me we had a Contorted Filbert in our yard. I pictured a scruffy guy recently fired from Cirque du Soleil standing out by the crepe myrtle with his leg wrapped around his head. Not criminal, but certainly unseemly for our neighborhood. I thought my wife was taking it awfully calmly. Then I saw her rolling out the garden hose and figured I'd better provide backup if she was going to start waterboarding some muscular French-Canadian hot-head from the circus. So I grabbed my axe handle and followed her out to the side of the house and saw her watering a wilted little tree whose limbs were . . . very . . . um . . . contorted.

Okay, so horticulture's not my strong suit. In fact, I feel like I've stumbled into foreign territory when I go to our neighborhood nursery, because they speak a language that's alien to me. "You could go with these colonoscopies, they've got nice catkins, but the plantar fasciitis won't need the sphagnum and duodenum mulch." You'd expect this from a professor using Power Point, but it's disconcerting coming from a manly dude with rough hands and a beard. Most guys don't really get into gardening until after their first marriage, when chasing women becomes more hazardous than fun. I remember the withering glares I'd get from the ladies in my neighborhood when I was single. They'd glance at the positively-absolutely-undeniably-reliably dead perennials in my forsaken yard and look at me like I was Casey Anthony.

Anyway, it turns out that a Contorted Filbert is a little tree that's also called a corkscrew hazel, but it's most commonly known as—get this—Harry Lauder's Walking Stick. Wow. Quite a moniker for a twisted little shrub. Most plants can be ID'd by one or two words—dogwood, wisteria, nostrilhair, trachea, phlegmweed—but this little guy gets practically a whole sentence.

"Nice plants, Marv, what are they?"

"That's an Aunt Mable's Trumpet-Style

Hearing Aid in the front, and the one with the little white flowers is a Birdie Finklestein's Left-Handed Corset Pull."

I looked up Harry Lauder on Wikipedia, and it said, "The guy the Contorted Filbert is named after."

I made that up. He was the world's most famous singer/comedian back around World War I, and, as a Scotsman, he always appeared on stage in the traditional kilt and tam-o'-shanter and carried a twisted walking stick. So now you know . . . the REST . . . of the story.

I was inspired by that, since I can't tell a hydrangea from a cerebellum. So now I'm naming all our plants after famous people's stage props. In our front yard we have a plant with purple leaves that's now a Lady Gaga's Meat Dress. By the deck in the back is a row of spindly things with shiny leaves that kind of lean to one side, commonly known around here as Elvis Presley's Bell Bottoms. Our Pete Townshend's Busted Guitar is flowering nicely, and I think the Alice Cooper's Python Vine will cover the side of the garage in another year.

My wife is not entirely onboard with the new labeling system, but knows I won't move as quickly if she tells me to water the variegated hostas. "Ohhhh," I'll exclaim after wandering past them a couple of times. "You mean the Janet Jackson Nipple Rings!"

The new system has certainly made my trips to the nursery more entertaining, albeit a tad longer. The other day it took the guy forever to find a flower I was looking for. Turned out they'd put some stupid Latin name on the Boy George Feather Boas.

DO YOU OVULATE HERE OFTEN?

Researchers at a Texas university say men can tell by smell alone when women are at their most fertile, and that women can usually tell by smell alone if a man is not interested in having sex, depending on how long he's been dead. The scientists reached their conclusion after getting men to sniff T-shirts worn by women during fertile and infertile stages of their menstrual cycles, and reported that about a third of the men participating assumed the T-shirts would be occupied and asked if there was a two-drink minimum.

The men overwhelmingly picked the T-shirts worn during the fertile phase as being more "pleasant" and "sexy." The study didn't reveal why men can sense such subtle differences in women's smells almost immediately, but can't find an anchovy pizza under a couch for two weeks.

For unexplained reasons, the T-shirt sniffers were right on target. "It may be a cue that men pick up subtly," said Devendra Singh, the psychologist at the University of Texas in Austin who made the discovery. Singh, the son of Billy Wayne and Thelma Jo Singh of Lubbock, said the findings shed light on how our ancestors selected mates before the Wonderbra evolved.

Singh said he doesn't think smell would play as important a role as visual cues in determining sexual attractiveness in today's society, which is no doubt a relief to Donna Karan. If smell were suddenly as important as visual cues, it would throw everything out of whack. For example, hiring dancers at gentlemen's clubs would get terribly complicated: "The greased inner-tube number was absolutely inspired, Nadine, really. But your Reproductive Olfactory Stimulation Response is a tad lackluster." I don't think we'll be seeing "Fertile-Smelling Babes" in neon any time soon.

Women obviously care about smells a lot more than men do. This is evidenced by the fact that the men's fragrance selection in a department store can be completely blocked from view by a single large shopper, whereas the women's fragrance department has its own alderman. Plus the obvious fact that men can sleep soundly in a room where a pile of gym socks and fast-food containers is busily producing compost, while most women would either pass out or crawl to the nearest exit.

In grad school I rented a house with two other guys, and we seemed to have an unmentioned competition over who could care less about domestic hygiene. One of my roommates once proudly showed me a chicken wing that had mummified behind his dresser. Once I found a sponge by the kitchen sink that had actually sprouted something with leaves. We were disgusting, as most of our rare female guests would point out before suddenly remembering they had to be somewhere clean. The "take charge" types would actually start to scour, say, the bathroom, then unearth some indescribable horror, scream, and evacuate. The premises, I mean. Men need far less bathroom storage space than women do, since all the unguents and emollients we require fit in a tube of Chapstick. So, upon investigating, we'd invariably find that she'd opened a drawer or a cabinet door that, as far as we knew, had never been opened, allowing wildlife to thrive.

So, given the rank horrors most men can tolerate, this discovery in Texas is doubly amazing—first, that men's sniffers are so sensitive, and, B, that an "aroma cue" can actually impact sexual attraction, like having four beers.

But guys, if you use this new inside information, there's a right and wrong way. Right: "Mmm, you smell divine. Is that a fragrance or just 'Naturally You'?"

Wrong: "Wow. Of all the women I've smelled tonight, you smell the most fertile."

The News and Ugly Rumors (NUR)

I got a degree in journalism, and my first real job was as a newspaper reporter. I knew I wanted to be a writer, and figured that was the only practical way to make a living at it while supporting my eating habit. So, years later, when I finally got a chance to write comedy, naturally I gravitated to satirical news stories—jokester journalism. I've written hundreds for TV shows and Premiere Radio Networks. Naturally, some aren't as fresh as they were when I wrote them. But I haven't included them for their news value, and I think the jokes have stood the test of time. Hope you do, too.

Tampa (NUR)—The National Right to Life Committee, which opposes abortion for any reason, declared today that life technically begins with lubrication. The decision was a compromise between moderate members who argue that life begins with penetration, and hard-liners who insist that life begins with the suggestion to slip into something more comfortable.

Washington (NUR)—Did famed flyer Amelia Earhart and her navigator die of thirst on a tiny island, as some experts claim, or did Earhart beat him to death with a pipe wrench after he said, "Is it hot enough for you?" one too many times? New evidence has rekindled the heated debate. One expert dismisses the discovery of a size-nine woman's shoe on the island, saying Earhart's navigator had probably said something like, "I'll bet you can't hit that island with your shoe," knowing Earhart couldn't resist a dare.

The Magic Fat Pill

No wonder everybody's so excited about the big medical announcement from Baylor College of Medicine in Houston, where genetic researchers said they've paved the way for a drug to be developed that would allow men to spontaneously look like George Clooney and know What Every Woman Wants.

No, wait. I'm sorry, wrong fantasy file. Now where did I put . . . oh, yes, here it is: the drug would allow you to eat like a pig, not exercise, and still lose weight. Shortly after the announcement, a Hollywood fundraiser for the project raised $137 million in twelve minutes. And no wonder: its impact on our culture would be radical, like legislating free beer for all males who wear caps.

The researcher who led the study (whose name is spelled entirely with the letters k and v and the symbol for magnesium) said the discovery could be an important step in the battle against obesity, a killer epidemic that is sweeping America but, mercifully, has so far not spread to Bangladesh, which has enough problems. Studies show that at least 70 million Americans are obese, including more than a third of all adults, one in five children, and approximately everyone who shops at my giant discount store. Obesity increases the risk of illness and death due to diabetes, heart disease, and sinking in fresh asphalt, but dramatically lowers the risk of dating a troubled fashion model.

While the gene-altering technique would be an important tool in treating obesity, the scientist said, it would be "great" for the guys who never exercise but like to sit on the couch and watch TV and drink beer and eat vast quantities of potato chips, meaning, of course, that it would be great for America. A leading couch potato on my block said such a drug would be "okay," but what would really be "great" would be a drug that makes bathroom trips unnecessary, because sometimes when he's in a hurry it feels uncomfortably like exercise. On the other hand, if he goes when he first feels the need, he has to leave the couch two or even three times during a televised sporting event, which for him approaches aerobic conditioning.

If the discovery pans out and people can in fact become inert pigs without putting on weight, the changes in Western civilization will no doubt be dramatic. Thousands of health-related businesses like fitness centers and health food companies will go belly up, excuse the expression, while Twinkie stock will skyrocket, candy "bars" will become candy "bricks," and your 346-pound Happy Meal will come with a Mini Cooper.

With everyone svelte, even six-foot, 89-pound pouting Swedes will look fleshy, so clothing companies will have to make robot runway models out of Tinkertoys. "The fat kid" will disappear from TV and movies unless the industry can get special permission to raise them on ranches.

And of course our beloved social order—which isn't overly orderly in the best of times—will be rent asunder. Consider all the pudgy people who won't go out to get the paper in the morning until after Johnny Jockstrap has jogged by. They hide in the garage to avoid having to wave their big, jiggly arms at him and flashing that fake, cholesterol-eating grin. But after the brains at Baylor unleash their gene-whammy on the world, the flat-tummied former fatties will get up early just so they can set up a La-Z-Boy in the driveway: "Morning, Johnny!" they'll yell, waving a slab of sausage pizza at him. "Want some breakfast? I don't have any Evian, but if you want a slug of this double Oreo milkshake you're welcome to it, buddy! Don't kink a ligament!"

It'll be a new day. Treadmills will become as quaint as rotary phones, Oprah will have to develop another obsession to bravely overcome, and I'll never again have to complain to a flight attendant that the passenger next to me is slopping over and occupying $200 worth of my seat.

And, perhaps most satisfying of all, there will be no reason for Richard Simmons to appear on TV in his underwear.

MOTEL 5

The first time I heard Tom Bodett's comforting, down-home drawl on the hilarious radio commercials he voices for Motel 6, I thought, "This is just begging for a parody." For a couple of years I wrote one a week and my comedy partner Jamie Alcroft voiced it. It became a favorite on the dozens of radio stations that aired it.

MOTEL 5: "Give Us Your Insufferable Passengers"

"Hi, I'm Tom Bidet for Motel 5, the cheapest accommodations you can find this side of a bench at the bus station. And speaking of which, if you're on one of them bus tours where you're crammed in with the same salt-of-the-earth bunch for a week, it can get awful tiresome listening to a salesman tell you the 437 pitfalls of purchasing the wrong road-grading equipment, or a recent divorcee's blow-by-blow account of those last few months with that miserable hairball. Well, just pull your bus into Motel 5, and give us the names of the two biggest bores on the bus. We have a special trade-off deal with the local pharmacies, and for no extra charge we'll see to it that the offending parties oversleep at least twelve hours to give you time to put a couple of states between you and the bore-weevils. What a deal, and only at Motel 5. We'll leave the seat up for you."

MOTEL 5: "Wade On Inn"

"Hi, I'm Tom Bidet for Motel 5, where you can get a clean, comfortable pair of rubber boots to wear in your room until we can get these plumbing problems taken care of. If you're like me, you don't spend much time on the floor of your motel room anyway. You're either propped up in bed with the TV remote, or taking a shower, where you're already wet. Well, we've got the remote unit conveniently chained to the wall by the bed, and we'd urge you to use it for all your television needs. It's just not a good idea to be wading around and monkeying with electric appliances. It has a tendency to blow the main transformer so *nobody* can watch television. And, in our experience, the next of kin is rarely a pleasant individual to deal with. So save yourself a bundle and slide on in to Motel 5. We'll leave the seat up for you."

ONE-MAN AVALANCHE

I drove through the mountains recently, and was reminded of the time I kicked off our summer vacation by nearly killing my parents. Now part of family lore, the episode was a knee-buckling example of the adage that God watches over morons.

I grew up on in a marshy area on the Mississippi Gulf Coast that was as flat as a mud puddle. We used to go to a construction site and play on a 20-foot-high pile of dirt, which was the highest point of land I'd ever seen until the fifth grade. When I was 12 and my brother was 10, our parents took us to the Smoky Mountains. The terrain was as mind-bogglingly alien to us as Jupiter's moons. We couldn't process the fact that we could look up and see rocks a half a mile up in the sky. As soon as we motored into the mountains, we started begging Dad to let us climb one, and he finally pulled into a rest stop and said Be Careful. We sprinted to the base of a mountain and began our assault.

When we got about 150 feet up, Mom yelled, "Hey, boys!" We turned and saw her holding the old Brownie. She took a picture. Fantastic. We'd have photographic evidence to show our fellow swamp rats that we'd actually climbed a mountain. After we'd gone maybe 50 yards higher, my dad yelled, "That's high enough, boys." We sat there 100 yards above the parking lot, savoring the moment. Being a boy, savoring got old quickly. I had to do something with the moment. I noticed a roundish rock about the size of a small washtub, so I braced against a tree and shoved with my legs and found I could make it jiggle. I said to my brother, "Let's see if this rock will make it all the way to the bottom of the hill."

Understand that this was the first mountain I had ever actually touched, so I knew nothing about the physics involved. Back home, to get something that big and heavy to go anywhere at all was a major project involving men and even machinery, and I was a skinny 12-year-old. My brother declined to help, being a future judge with better judgment than I. So I shoved and strained against that brute until it started down the hill, and I immediately saw that it wasn't just going to make it to the bottom—it might make it to Gatlinburg.

I screamed, "Daddy!" and my poor dad looked up to see a 200-pound battering ram screaming down that mountain like a runaway train, headed for cars, kids, families. He ran around screaming for everybody to get out of the way and then watched helplessly as that rock—now going probably 60 miles per hour—missed our car by about six feet, bounced across the parking lot, and disappeared into the woods on the other side after hitting . . . nothing. It was a minor miracle, like firing a shotgun in a crowded room and finding the only two-foot gap where nobody stood. My mom sobbed into her hands. My dad leaned on the car to keep his legs from collapsing under him. I looked at my brother, who was looking at me with an expression that was easy to read: "Dead man walking."

I knew exactly what was waiting for me. I climbed down very slowly to give my Mom as much time as possible to remind Dad that he had wanted children, and to give Dad some time to cool down so his response would be measured. The belt stung, but he didn't cross the line into child abuse. He just made real sure that there was one particular lesson in rock technology that I will never, ever, ever forget.

Politically Incorrect with Bill Maher

I'm really dating myself here, but way back when Bill Maher got his big break and his cable show was brought over to ABC from Comedy Central, he asked me if I'd come write for him. Bill had always really loved my sense of humor and we enjoyed each other, and of course he wanted to surround himself with writers he liked and that could deliver the goods. He knew this was his big shot and he didn't want to blow it, and of course I was honored that he picked me to join his staff of seven guys.

I found out after a couple of months that I'm too much of a performer to go into a cubicle for 9 hours a day five days a week. And I hated the fact that about 98% of what all of us wrote was tossed out, and we're talking about a lot of really great stuff. I wasn't happy—I called it going to the coal mine—so I left as soon as I qualified for my Writer's Guild Health Insurance for the year!

But while I was there I admit it was fun getting my jokes on the air. I started out as a newspaper reporter, so I knew how to pull stuff from the news and turn it into jokes.

When I first started, I got really frustrated because I was writing what I thought were great monologue jokes, and Bill just wasn't picking them. So I studied the jokes that were getting into the monologue and finally realized what was happening.

By nature I'm not an edgy or mean comedian. I like to do down-home, family-friendly comedy, and it showed. In a word, I wasn't being MEAN enough. After I figured that out, I'd go in and get into this nasty, mean persona that wasn't really me, but hey, he hired me to write jokes he'd do on the air and that was the only way I could do it.

Herewith, some of my "scores," or jokes that he performed in his opening monologue.

(President Bill Clinton was being sued)
In the Paula Jones sexual harassment case, the Supreme Court was considering today whether a President can be sued while he's in office, and if residents have to be notified when a former Arkansas governor moves into their neighborhood.

Female fish in a north Florida river are developing male sex organs, and it's blamed on waste from a paper mill. It's so sad when a male fish is trapped inside a female's body.

(Gingrich was the Republican Speaker of the House and made some embarrassing comments that were picked up on the airwaves)
The lawyer for the Florida couple who taped the infamous Newt Gingrich conference call off a police scanner said his clients "did the right thing" even though they might have violated federal law. Gingrich's attorney responded angrily, saying, "Damn it, that's our story."

(Gingrich was in financial trouble)
The House of Representatives voted today to reprimand Newt Gingrich and fine him $300,000.

Gingrich said he'd be happy to pay the fine because he needs the tax deduction.

President Clinton officially began his second term yesterday, and insiders said he was relieved to have another chance because there were so many promises from the first campaign that he didn't get around to breaking.

(*Yeltsin was a Soviet leader*)
Boris Yeltsin has called for a higher tax on vodka to try to do something about Russia's drinking problem. He said he decided to do something about it when the last big military parade in Red Square turned into a conga line.

(*This one has a story. Bill closed the monologue with it on a Wednesday—the "closer" is the joke he considers the best of the day—but ABC's lawyers said the way it was worded could invite lawsuits so they cut it from the show, which infuriated Bill. I re-worded it and he closed the monologue with it the next day*)
A jury awarded the Food Lion Supermarket chain five and a half million dollars in that lawsuit against this network, saying ABC used illegal means to videotape rat-gnawed cheese and unsafe food handling. So ABC was forced to eat a little crow . . . which at Food Lion is marked "Cornish Hen."

(*A commercial featured the famous dancer*)
Green Bay won the Super Bowl by 14 points, exactly as the bookies predicted. There were a couple of surprises: Desmond Howard returned a kick-off to dance in the end zone, and Fred

Astaire returned from the dead to dance with a vacuum cleaner.

(*AOL had been having massive technical problems and thousands of customers were in an uproar*)
Clinton said every classroom should be connected to the Internet, which he called "our new town square," if they can get past America Online, which he called "our new village idiot."

(*It had been an extremely rough road for the unconvicted murderer*)
On the way home after the verdict, OJ stopped at an ice cream parlor. He got a little agitated when the guy behind the counter said, "Rocky Road?"

(*Simpson couldn't explain why traces of blood were in his clothing*)
As jurors in the Simpson trial tried to decide on punitive damages, Simpson's attorneys said, "You can't get blood out of a turnip." OJ said he wasn't surprised—he couldn't even get it out of his socks.

(*Ron Goldman's parents sued for civil damages over their son's death*)
As jurors in the Simpson trial tried to decide on punitive damages, OJ claimed a net worth of less than zero. The Goldmans said they appreciated him finally admitting it, but they were talking about money.

Avis Rent-a-Car, already being sued for discriminating against blacks, is now accused of discriminating against Jews. A spokesman said it was just a misunderstanding of a promotion that offered "free upgrades, free fill-ups, and a country ham to our uncircumcised customers."

A federal task force has been formed to find more respectful ways to notify families of air crash victims, after some got the news on answering machines and even in the media. They'll also require airlines to pay full refunds and not pro-rate for how far they made it.

A Milwaukee couple is looking for a woman to conceive a grandchild for them using the frozen sperm of their late son, who died several years ago. Meanwhile, family members have asked them to stop wearing their t-shirts that say, "Have I shown you the pictures of my son's sperm?"

*A rare hat trick—I had three scores in a single day!**

(*Clarence Thomas had been accused of lewd behavior with an employee*)
*The Supreme Court heard arguments about indecent material on the Internet. Sandra Day O'Connor asked if the Internet could be compared to a telephone, and Clarence Thomas asked how to find the website that shows "white chicks with big butts."

*Mexico's drug-fighting reputation took another beating as drug tests in the attorney general's office found 241 police agents with cocaine, pot, and other drugs in their systems.

The cops claimed they were just storing evidence in their kidneys.

*Former Congressman Wes Cooley of Oregon was convicted of falsely claiming in a voter pamphlet that he served with the Special forces in Korea. He said it was a misunderstanding. He meant to say he served the Specials in a Korean restaurant.

(*Before a national competition, figure skater Tonya Harding's boyfriend hired a "hitman" to smash her rival, Nancy Kerrigan, on the knee with a hammer*)
Hospital records show figure skater Oksana Baiul was driving under the influence of alcohol at the time of last weekend's car crash in Hartford. Baiul says she's the victim, because Tonya Harding got her hammered.

(*After giving police investigators a ton of damaging information about O.J. Simpson, at trial she claimed she "forgot" everything she had said.*)
At the big TV programming convention in new Orleans, an announcement that yet another player in the OJ trial is getting her own show. A cable channel announced that Rosa Lopez will host a program called "Unsolved Memories."

(*An investigation showed the Swiss didn't take valuables from Jews when they were being taken to death camps*)
Israel and the Palestinians finally reached a hard-fought agreement on a partial Israeli withdrawal from Hebron. Calls were made to President Clinton and the king of Jordan for

their help, and to Switzerland thanking them for not ripping off the Jews while they were busy.

At a House hearing into cellular phone eavesdropping, a Louisiana congressman used a piece of wire and a soldering gun to convert a legal scanner into one that would pick up other calls. Then, just to show off, he used a bottle cap and a remote control to give Dick Armey "itchy pants."

(*China apparently illegally contributed to Gore's campaign*)
China signed major deals with the U.S. to buy planes and build cars, and as they toasted, Al Gore sloshed champagne on the floor. Aides say he was just nervous: He's not used to taking money from the Chinese with everybody watching.

Parents complained that sexual images on cable aren't scrambled enough, so the Supreme Court ruled they have to be completely scrambled or stay off until after 10 pm. Parents say they just ran out of explanations as to why naked ladies like popsicles so much.

(*A ValuJet plane crashed in the Everglades killing 105*)
ValuJet has hired one of the nation's most prestigious ad agencies to help create a new image. A spokesman said they fired their old agency when the best slogan they could come up with was, "What are the chances of it happening twice?"

STAR STRUCK—REPEATEDLY

I don't mean to brag, but I think I might hold the world's record for getting pummeled by famous people. The paparazzi don't qualify, because they're jerks and should be flogged daily. And they shouldn't be allowed to win anything.

I practiced karate in college and once competed in a big tournament in Dallas. Coincidentally, the referee for my obscure little match happened to be Chuck Norris—the then-reigning U.S. Karate Champion who went on to become an action star.

I was good with my feet, and could nail a guy in the gut with a roundhouse kick before he could move his arms to block it. But Texans thought kicks were for sissies and real men scored with their fists. I got mad because the judges wouldn't award me points for my gorgeously executed kicks, even though Stevie Wonder would have *sensed* their undeniable beauty and raised a Point flag. So I lost my head and went after my opponent with fists a-flyin' and ignored Mr. Norris' order to "Stop!" Bad move. He grabbed me by the collar of my gi and marched me across the ring kicking my butt for emphasis: "When I say STOP (BAM!), I mean STOP (BAM!)." I chose not to fight back, because on my list of "People Not to Pick Fights With" the current U.S. Karate Champion is perennially in the Top One. So when I was still a teenager, my butt cheeks had already been reddened by the star of nine seasons of *Walker, Texas Ranger.*

My comedy partner and I had a TV series last century, a sketch show called *Comedy Break with Mack & Jamie,* and every episode had hilarious guests from Leslie Nielsen to John Larroquette; but only one who drew blood. Richard Moll, the huge guy who played "Bull" on Night Court, was my server in "The S & M Diner," where "the waiters smack your lips for you" and they serve "black and blue-eyed peas," etc. He said, "A little something before dinner?" I nodded, and the quick fore- and backhand SLAP-SLAP to my jaw was so hard it crossed my eyes. When the director yelled Cut, Richard said, "That wasn't too hard, was it?"

I smiled, said, "Well, I'm still conscious," and spit blood into a napkin.

But my greatest claim to fame for being battered by the rich and famous occurred in Key West, where Jamie and I teamed up. After we had done a few TV appearances, we were invited back to host the annual Fantasy Fest costume contest. Our job was to bring the contestants on stage, get as many laughs as possible, and get them off again. Tennessee Williams was one of the many celebs who had a house on the island, and he loved a good time and thought sobriety was vastly overrated.

After hustling Number 36 offstage, we saw that Number 37 was a grinning world-renowned playwright being wrangled by a tanned and muscular young man, his "assistant" for the evening. Williams was dressed in a black-and-white *keffiyeh*—an Arab headdress—sunglasses, and a white robe and was carrying a curved, six-foot shepherd's staff. He was grinning blissfully, having apparently started Happy Hour just after breakfast. The crowd cheered when we brought him on. Williams paraded around the stage, enjoying the adulation of the crowd, and Jamie got a laugh saying he was responsible for the high price of gasoline.

Then I stepped downstage and said, "Looks like Yasser Arafat and Little Bo Peep had a love child!" and WHAM! something hard hit me between the shoulder blades, nearly knocking me offstage. I had been struck with a shepherd's staff by a double Pulitzer-Prize-winner! Jamie said, "Now, that's why there'll never be peace in the Middle East," and Williams clobbered him. He was doing it in fun, not anger, and the crowd loved it. We ad-libbed a bit more as we steered him offstage and got him safely back into the ripped arms of his assistant.

Later, over drinks with friends, I wondered aloud if "physically assaulted by Tennessee Williams" would punch up our résumé.

"That could be your hook," said our friend B.J., pointing to a big guy at the bar wearing a tropical shirt, sunglasses and using a cigarette holder. "How about 'Knocked cold as a flounder by Hunter S. Thompson'?"

Tempting. But since our jaws had to be in working order to do the act, we declined.

THE NEWS AND UGLY RUMORS

NEW YORK (NUR)—The FBI said today the foreign terrorists who were plotting to blow up New York's Holland Tunnel not only mistakenly thought the Wall Street area would be flooded, but also thought the tunnel went to Holland.

In addition to attacking New York, mastermind Assem Hammoud intended to strike a blow at "the infidel dogs who created the cartoon of Muhammed," an FBI spokesman said. When informed that he had confused the Dutch with the Danes, Hammoud became despondent and activated a hidden belt armed with Diet Coke and Mentos. He drowned in the ensuing torrent, becoming the first known victim of a suicide effervescing.

Hammoud's mentor, Afghan jihad leader Mustafah Said, released a statement saying he would be carefully reviewing all applications for "mastermind" to ensure that other applicants possessed the basic requirement of a mind.

VIETNAM (NUR)—A father has agreed to change his son's name from Fined Six Thousand and Five Hundred—the amount he was forced to pay in local currency for ignoring Vietnam's two-child policy. Local government officials tried for years to persuade Mai Xuan Can to change the boy's name because classmates constantly teased him. Can finally relented, changing his son's name to Local Government Officials Gargle Pig Vomit.

SECRET SURROGATE (NUR)—In Boston, sperm and an egg from anonymous donors were united and placed in the womb of an unnamed surrogate mother who had the child for an unidentified couple who couldn't find the unnamed hospital where the anonymous surrogate mother allegedly gave birth to their as yet undiscovered child, unconfirmed sources report.

FUNNY FURRY FELLOW TRAVELERS

Fair warning: this column contains a description of a ferret doing something you might not want in your memory banks.

There's just nothing funnier to humans than seeing animals in wacky situations or exhibiting outlandish, usually human-like behavior. Somebody just sent me the YouTube link to Mishka the Talking Husky. Off-camera, Mishka's owners coo, "I looooove you, Mishka." And after a few prompts, Mishka very clearly howls, "Iiiii uhhhh woooo. Owwwww. Iiiii uhhh woooo."

I must be jaded. The Pledge of Allegiance would have impressed me, but to me, "talking" requires an occasional consonant. I would have been happy with, "All aboard for Hoboken," but "iiii uhhh oooo" didn't fire a single endorphin for me. I can ask my dog how I like my oysters, and she'll say "Raw! Raw! Raw!" but that doesn't make her an orator.

I prefer the pure-entertainment animal videos that make no lofty claims, like the dancing cockatoo, the poodle in the conga line, the skateboarding bulldog. What's so cute and hilarious to us is that they'll do it for fun or a single treat, which we also find precious because the average human won't get off the couch for a single bite of anything: "Stand all the way up for a Cheeto? Nah. How about a Big Mac?"

We were visiting my aunt and uncle one day when suddenly, "KA-WHONG!" a loud gonging crash sent a shockwave through the house. As my parents and I exchanged an alarmed look, my aunt and uncle exchanged a tired one.

"Bo's hungry," explained my uncle. Their bovine mixed-breed dog Bo had had a bad habit of dragging his plastic bowl all over the yard and they'd have to hunt it down at mealtime. My uncle nailed it to the porch, and Bo promptly chewed it into an abstract colander-like sculpture. So they got a fifteen-pound iron bowl that Bo could neither drag nor chew. The brute could lift the thing about a foot and a half, however, and when it hit the wooden porch from that height, it shook the windows and alerted the inhabitants that he could go for a nibble.

Odd animal behavior came up at a party recently. Someone smiled at a mutual friend and said, "Have you heard about C's ferret?" I confessed I hadn't, so C told the story. Seems the ferret fell in love with a mop and would drag it upstairs by its "hair" and make mad, frenetic, Pepé Le Pew love to it a couple times a day. Ferrets belong to the same family as minks, so insert your own joke here.

I thought, "What an insane animal." Then it occurred to me that, on the other hand, the mop never had a headache or pouted, and gift holidays slid past it unnoticed. It didn't interrogate the ferret about where it had been, or why it friended an old girlfriend on Facebook, or even care if the ferret was seeing another mop. It didn't require dinner to get in the mood, or ask no-win questions about the size of its butt. Then it occurred to me that my wife was going to read this, and that I had better remind her that my job is to write jokes, so sometimes I have to imagine what it's like for all those unlucky guys out there who don't have a perfect mate like I do. Then I bought her a little something "just because" and made reservations at an extortionately expensive restaurant.

THE RIGHT TO BARE GREEN ARMS

I hope you had a fun Halloween, my favorite holiday, when witches roam the earth and insurance adjusters wear pantyhose on their heads.

I love Halloween because it's our only guilt-free holiday. In-laws don't whine about who had dinner where last year, there's no stressing over gifts, and the less devout aren't obliged to feel even more heathenish than usual.

No, it's the lively night when toddlers are dressed as pandas and bunnies, kids joyfully smear themselves with fake blood, and grown-ups make complete fools of themselves because society has given us a freebie—Mardi Gras for the rest of us. A soccer mom can dress as a slutty vampire for a night and won't be ostracized by the carpool. A bearded factory worker can don a mini-skirt and a bra stuffed with volleyballs and it might actually burnish his reputation at work: "You shoulda seen Billy Wayne, Lord, he's a wild man. Last I seen him a leopard woman had her tail around him and they was doin' the dirty boogaloo."

The frustrations of phone menus, rude drivers, plugged bridges and brain-dead politicians push us toward the edge of insanity all year, and Halloween gives us the opportunity to actually cross that border for a few blissful hours and not suffer dire consequences. Thus, "It was Halloween, Your Honor," is considered by many to be a legitimate alibi.

Young men appreciate the fact that Halloween transforms many otherwise modest young ladies into brazen exhibitionists. That prim receptionist suddenly has license to reveal her inner pole dancer, and portions of her anatomy rarely seen in public are not only lasciviously displayed but are painted green. You don't get that at Thanksgiving. If you do, it's a clear call for a change in medication.

I like the fact that there are still some mysteries associated with the night of ghosts and goblins. For example, I have no idea what a goblin is. It sounds like something that might eat too fast, but there's nothing really scary about a messy shirt-front and heartburn.

Another unknown is how werewolves and vampires get along. Some say they hate each other, but I suspect that's the vial-half-empty crowd. There are such huge differences between them that I doubt it's ever an issue—like asking how poor black lesbians get along with Republicans. Vampires are generally elegantly dressed and do well at parties, whereas werewolves run naked and have fleas, automatically disqualifying them from most black-tie functions.

Another difference: a werewolf will use a crucifix as a chew-toy, but show one to a vampire and he cringes in fear. Which is why you never hear of a vampire problem in Catholic neighborhoods—crucifixes everywhere. He gets the sweater off, he opens the blouse, he's about to chomp on the neck and AAUURGH! There it is on a gold chain, ruining dinner.

So many delicious mysteries among the things that go bump and chomp and "Dude!" in the night. Take advantage while you can. They already make us wear seatbelts and helmets and refuse us service if we don't wear shoes and shirts. What's next? Taking away our inalienable right to wear a pink tutu, a snakeskin leotard, flamenco jacket, and a Mitch McConnell mask? I don't think it'll happen, because now more than ever, the powers know we need a little insanity.

Fun Country Songs

I've listened to and sung country music all my life, and since I like to bang on the guitar, naturally I've written some country songs designed to tickle your funny-bone.

On stage I've gotten laughs with some country song titles I've written that are pretty hokey, but hey, we're here to have fun, right? Here's a sampling:

"I Still Believe It's Noble, Living In A Home That's Mobile"

"I Wish I'd Known Up Front, How Much Behind You'd Get"

"You're The Blue Light Special Of My K-Mart Life"

"I Got Tears In My Beer 'Cause There's Stickers In My Knickers."

"I Thought I'd Lost Her Forever, Then Somehow The Witch Got Paroled"

"You've Got The Cutest Pair I've Ever Seen, Guess I'm A Mudflap Man."

I actually made a silly video of this one, although I didn't include the spoken intro that I used to do when

I'd do it live at parties and such. To see the video, go to YouTube, type my name in the Search box, and it should come up on the list of my videos. If not, type in the title.

I DON'T RESPECT YOU NOW

(*Spoken intro*) Back in my single days, I was out one night and I got to dancing with this cute young thing and we seemed to be hitting it off pretty good, so I bought her a drink, and we danced a little more, and after awhile I figured the time was right so I asked her if she'd like to go home with me, and I made a little joke. I said, "That is, if you'll respect me in the morning." Well, she looked at me kinda funny and then she said, "In the morning? Heck, I don't respect you now." Well, I went home—alone—and since I had some time on my hands I wrote this song.

Well I woke up Sunday morning,
and I couldn't believe my eyes.
The beauty that took me home last night
looked like one of the guys!
It 'bout scared me to death when she opened
    her eyes,
I nearly jumped right outa my skin,
I swear I didn't mean to knock her cold as a
    wedge,
But my knee hit one of her chins!
(I shoulda said:)

    (CHORUS)
    Thank you for the offer,

But I'll get by somehow.
Never mind about in the mornin',
I don't respect you now.
You see, I don't wanta do nothin'
I'll have to lie about anyhow,
So to hell with in the mornin', girl,
I don't respect you now.

Well the dance hall late next Friday night was a
    desperation zone.
Tag team elimination to see who was goin' home
    alone.
A girl was making the rounds and gettin' turned
    down,
She even tried all the guys in the band.
Then she spotted something weak and helpless,
And she knew that I was her man,
    (why didn't I say)

    (CHORUS)

You know a man's gotta do what a man's gotta do,
I'm no exception to the rule.
I went huntin' for a little bit of TLC,
Guess I'm stubborn as a mule.
Through the smoke and the gloom I saw her
    workin' the room,
Til she finally settled for me.
But then something she said flipped a switch in
    my head and finally set me free,
'cause I said

    (CHORUS and FADE)

COMEDY BREAK WITH MACK AND JAMIE

I've been in the comedy team of Mack & Jamie since 1980, and at this writing Jamie and I still work occasionally but we've both moved on to solo pursuits. Back in the day, we had a syndicated TV show called Comedy Break with Mack & Jamie. *We shot 125 half-hour episodes in a few months, which was insane, but we had a lot of loyal fans who loved our brand of smart silliness. You can go on YouTube and find a lot of our sketches. Just type in* Comedy Break *or Mack and Jamie and a bunch of stuff will come up.*
One of the things I came up with was a spoof of a hick TV commercial for "Buford's House of Liver." It was a great template, so our writer Buddy Sheffield would come up with two or three we could do every week to the same hokey tune, always selling something totally off-the-wall and hilarious. Jan Hooks and I would dress in these hideously outdated outfits and sing as country-corny as possible, and people loved it.
Decades after Comedy Break *folded, I did a solo video version of "Buford's" and you can see it if you type in Buford's House of Liver or my name in the YouTube search box.*

BUFORD'S HOUSE OF LIVER

If your wife has been cooking her fangers to
the bone,

There's a wonderful treat you can give her
  (*give her*)
Git out of your rut, come and stuff your
  hungry gut
Down at Buford's House of Liver.

At Buford's House of Liver, our meat will
  make you quiver,
It's prepared with love and with pride
  (*with pri-i-i-de*)
You'll never see a liver-lover judge a cow by
  its cover,
'Cause the best parts are all deep inside.

(SPOKEN) How many times have you said
to yourself, "Boy, I could sure go for some
animal innards tonight, but I just don't want
to slave over a hot stove"? Well, come on down
to Buford's House of Liver, conveniently located
just past where Lonnie's Body Shop used to be
before it burned down, about a mile and a half
past where the blacktop ends. And if you're in
the mood for seafood, let our renowned liver
sculptor, Leonard Barger, carve your liver into
the fish of your choice.

If you're looking to find a place that's one
  of a kind
Only one place we know can deliver,
  (*liver*)
Come see Buford and Leonard for the best-
  tastin' innards,
Down at Buford's House of Liver
Buford's House of Liver

BAYOU SELF

I haven't made a video of this one, but I recorded it with my wacky-funny and very versatile musician friend Eddie Baytos, who pulled in some favors and got some great performances from some musician friends for me. I put swamp sounds over it—frogs, crickets, gators grunting, birds squawking, and it sounds great. I sure have enjoyed singing it over the years. I know you can't feel the foot-stompin' energy by reading it, but I'll bet you get a couple of grins.

I ain't got no catfish, I ain't got no greens,
I ain't had a woman, since I left New
   Orleans,
If the beans and bugs don't kill me
Then the weather surely will,
But the law won't never find me,
I bet a hundred dollar bill.

(CHORUS)

Ain't nobody find you, livin' on the bayou
Livin' down on Bayou Self.
Bayou self, Bayou Self, livin' on the bayou
   by yo' self
Doin' what you wanta do,
Livin' like you want to
Livin' down Bayou Self.

Melissa said she loved me but she loved my
   best friend too,
So I borrowed all her money, took her car
   to Baton Rouge,
That's where I married sweet Sharlene
And where she broke my heart,

The judge said "Give her all you got!"
So I gave her my regards—"bye bye."

(CHORUS)

I raised some nice tomatoes,
They was big and fat and red,
Mr. Possum et 'em up last night,
so I et him up instead.
I got berries in the bushes,
I got crawfish in the pan,
I been on my knees most all my life
It's time I took my stand.

(CHORUS)

*I didn't record this verse, but I enjoyed writing it,
thought you'd smile:*

The sheriff come a-lookin', I let him chase
    me all around,
Last time that I seen him he was swimmin'
    for high ground,
His bloodhounds found a gator,
He ain't got no bloodhounds left,
He don't trouble me no more down here on
    Bayou Self.

(CHORUS)

*Then at the end while the swamp music kept
going and the crickets were scratching, I threw this
onto the end in a sing-songy chant:*

Black-eyed peas, n' cypress knees,
Muscadines, catfish lines,

Skeeter hawks, n' bugs that talks,
Gator grunt, possum hunt,
Loggerheads and hot cornbread,
Whisky still, drink your fill,
Coon dog songs, all night long, and *fade.*

ERIK THE RED, BJORN THE BEIGE

Hard to believe, but the 1,013[th] anniversary of the discovery of the New World is here, and consumers are all a-twitter about those Erikson Day, Millennial Blowout Sales. "In 999, Erikson sailed the ocean brine," as every school child knows.

The story actually began back in 960, when the great Norse explorer Erik the Red sailed off to find a warm island paradise and instead discovered Iceland, where summer usually occurs on the second Thursday in July.

Erik the Red's first mate, Gunter the Chartreuse, suggested they go find Hawaii or the Bahamas—someplace they didn't have to wear fur coats to the beach—but Erik the Red said those places were for sissy explorers like Bjorn the Beige and Lars the Lavender.

So he sailed off again and found another humongous island which he named Greenland, hoping his men wouldn't notice it was just as cold and miserable as Iceland.

Soon, however, his men realized that Greenland was actually named for the color your toes turn before you have to leave them on the tundra (from the Norse: *tun-*, or "God-forsaken," and *-dra*, "hell-hole").

After Erik retired, his son Leif (pronounced

"Leif") changed his last name from "The Red" to "Erik's Son" for credit purposes, later dropped the apostrophe because it was tacky, and became Leif Erikson, Unsung Real Discoverer of the New World.

Young Leif carried on his father's lifetime quest to find the most uncomfortable places on earth. Finally, after untold hardships, he Found a New Land he called New Found Land, all the creative types having frozen to death during the crossing.

So, in 999, some 450 years before Christopher Columbus was a nauseous look in his mother's eye, Erikson rode the boat ashore, Hallelujah, and set foot on the New World.

As the discoverer of a Brand New Place, Erikson had a duty to spread diseases, loot the land, and enslave the native populations. He was thus disappointed to find Newfoundland contained not one single peace-loving population to enslave. Deeming the rape and pillage prospects limited at best (some experts cite a species of red-bearded moose in Eastern Canada as evidence that at least some interaction occurred), Erikson ordered his men to dig a few foundations and scatter around some stuff that could be carbon dated later.

Then, certain that he would have a bank holiday or at the very least a city in Ohio named after him, Erikson left the New World and returned triumphantly to the Previously-Owned World, having secured his place in history as an annoying asterisk that would one day drive American History purists absolutely, stark-raving, betsy-bug crazy.

* * *

DETROIT (NUR)—Secret Service agents protecting the president are jumpy after two false alarms in recent days, and now comes word that a flasher in a raincoat was critically injured when an agent grabbed what he thought was a sawed off shotgun and wrestled it to the ground. "Honest mistake," the agent said. "It looked loaded to me."

Extensive reconstructive surgery was required to rehabilitate the injured flasher, who now goes by the name "Jeannine."

TERRIFYING LIES AND VICIOUS GREENS

Just because I don't play golf doesn't mean I think people who do are shallow or have misplaced priorities or waste half their lives in a vapid, worthless, meaningless activity. And if I did think that I certainly wouldn't say it out loud or write it in a column, because there are lots of perfectly normal people—Alice Cooper and Tiger Woods come to mind—who are devoted to golf, and most of them don't even dance with pythons or commit adultery with more women than live in Lithuania. Most of them are just normal people, like Donald Trump.

So I don't judge people who enjoy playing golf—they have every right to fritter away their lives however they want to. It's just that I have approximately nine million things I want to do before I burn the time required to get proficient at herding a little ball into a hole with sticks. Not that there's anything wrong with it. It's obviously a great game, judging by how many people watch it on TV. And since so many people watch it, the networks make gazillions broadcasting it, so the tournaments can attract the best golfers in the world to play for huge cash prizes, and the games are so tense ("terrifying approach," "fighting for his life," "nightmarish meltdown," "vicious green") and the stakes so high that advertisers pony up millions, which allows huge cash prizes and so on. And the great thing is that you can watch a round of golf in only four or five hours and don't have to waste your whole day.

The other great thing is that the action is literally non-stop, because there are dozens of guys playing on the same course, so they can cut from a guy wearing white pants standing and looking at his ball and then squatting and staring intently across the grass at the hole, to a guy wearing plaid pants standing and looking at his ball and then squatting and staring intently across the grass at the hole. And sometimes the action is so intense that you'll actually get a golfer raising his leg and pumping his fist! When that happens, everybody with a camera clicks like crazy, because that's the most explosive movement you're going to get out of a golfer all day, and will be the two-second "teaser" the network shows so you'll watch the highlights of the "action" on Sports Roundup later.

Oh, another great thing: During these televised tournaments they'll have little segments called "Swing Fix" and such. This is where one of the top athletes in the sport—usually a gray-haired guy with a doughy mid-section—demonstrates something to help you swing a club better. You just don't get that in other sports, because most guys watching at home have little need to hone their skills, for example, at kicking a guy in the throat, or blocking a 300-pound lineman, or fist-fighting while wearing ice skates.

Of course, that's still another great thing about the sport: you can play at any age (a Senior Tour in kickboxing or hockey would signal the end of our civilization even more certainly than, say, *Jersey Shore*). In fact, you don't have to go through the agony of getting in top physical condition to play it, even on the professional level! You can eat cheeseburgers and drink beer and smoke cigarettes all day long, and then go to the course the next day and make half a million dollars if you can whack a ball straight and waddle to the next hole! Must make all those boxers and football players feel pretty silly training their butts off six hours a day and watching their diets when some of their fellow professional athletes can have chili fries and a beer halfway through a practice round. Whoa. Wrong sport, Sport.

The final great thing about golf: when I need to refresh myself with a good nap, nothing transports me to Sleepyland quicker than tuning in to a tournament, pressing the Mute button, and watching four or . . . fi . . . .

60,000 YEARS OF PEACE, MUD AND MUSIC

Seems it couldn't be more than a millennium or so, but this month marks the 100,000[th] anniversary of the beginning of The Stone Age, billed by its Neanderthal organizers as "Sixty Thousand Years of Peace, Mud and Music."

Like most other great eras, this one began humbly, even by Paleolithic standards. One day, a few long-haired elders (you made Elder at 19 back then, when most medical treatment involved a scary-looking guy dancing around shaking bones) were sitting around, gnawing on bear meat, perhaps discussing who would be Lunch Bait the next day, when someone threw a bunch of dried hemp onto the campfire, and gradually the conversation turned whimsical.

After noting the amazing brilliance of the marmalade skies, one free-thinker had a notion: What if they threw an Age, and everybody went naked, sloshed around in the mud, smoked and ingested anything they wanted to, and did the horizontal boogaloo whenever, wherever, and with whomever they wanted?

The group thought it was a grand idea and celebrated by eating everything within a two-mile radius.

The Stone Age (not to be confused with The Rock Era) was named, of course, for the single ingredient found in most durable goods of the period: versatile and attractive stone, which was waterproof, shock-resistant, and, most importantly, everywhere, therefore making rock cartels impracticable. And, true to its long-lasting namesake, The Stone Age had a dazzling 60,000-year run for obvious reasons:

1. If you ate a plant that enabled you to see a girl with kaleidoscope eyes or even The Walrus, you could just sit back and enjoy it without fear of a surprise blood test at work. (*Downside: if the ivory-tusked Walrus you were grinning back at happened in fact to be a hungry saber-toothed tiger, you probably wouldn't be evolving with the rest of the group).

2. When the musicians started pounding those hollow logs and howling, you could get naked and dance in the mud 'til the mammoths came home, and nobody hassled you as long as you didn't sing louder than the band. (*Downside: drum solos sometimes lasted for days).

3. If you saw a fetching lass bending over, gathering berries, you didn't even have to say, "Excuse me, do you come to this flood plain often?" before contributing your charming brow ridge to the gene pool. (*Downside for the ladies: Back then, every gentleman caller was, well, a Neanderthal; so if you weren't into chinless guys with thick skulls and sloping foreheads, you either had to lower your standards, stay home every weekend, or wait for the Neolithic Age).

4. Incredible feasts grew on trees and wandered around in herds, and the portions were huge. (*Downside: Some creatures had not yet gotten the word that Man was atop the food chain, so exactly who would comprise the Dinner

Special was often decided only after a loud and ugly scene. Also, handling fire was still an iffy proposition, so if you were picky, you could starve to death waiting around for lightning to render your buffalo, say, medium well).

Everything has to come to an end, of course, and this party was no exception. Even the most venerable traditions: dancing naked, being filthy and semi-conscious, mating with the most human-looking mud lumps in the campsite—began to lose their novelty.

Eventually there were only a few old people sitting around talking about how great things were during The Good Old Age, before this fancy Bronze business started. How things were made to last back then, because their knives and spearheads and garlic presses and weed whackers were made out of real rock, like the gods intended, and not this sissy stuff the kids use today.

And the music back then! Whoa! Now that was the real thing: hard-driving, big-beat, whoop-and-holler music, not this sappy flute-and-harp stuff you can't even dance to.

So when somebody gets nostalgic for the Good Old Age and decides to throw a 100,000th Anniversary Stone Age Celebration, it'll no doubt result in a pale facsimile. Heck, there'll probably even be a dress code.

BERLIN (NUR)—The makers of RU-486, the so-called morning-after birth control pill, yesterday introduced RU-487, a so-called moments-before pill that makes women nauseous during heavy petting. While developing the drug, researchers noted that women lost interest in having sex almost immediately, while almost half the men lost interest if the woman was actually throwing up. Another third said it was annoying but not enough to stop, while about six percent said they were used to their partners throwing up during sex.

NEW YORK (NUR)—More organized crime figures have been arrested in a domino effect that started with the conviction of mob boss John Gotti, now in prison after stunning testimony by Salvatore "Sammy the Bull" Gravano. Recently indicted are Paul "Pauly the Animal" Scalina, Edward "Eddie the Viral Infection" Bengacci, Thomas "Tommy the Rabid Sewer Rat" Tosconi, and William "Billy the Bottom-Feeding Leech of Death" Mosanetti.

MOTEL 5: "Save On Christmas Shopping"

"Hi, I'm Tom Bidet for Motel 5, the cheapest accommodations you can find this side of a Salvation Army shelter. Here it is, time for decking the halls and jingle bells and a Ho Ho Ho and a bottle of rum to relieve the stress after a hard day at the mall. You're probably out there right now, running yourself ragged, standing at the checkout counter behind some mental elf who's buying enough stuff to fill the stockings of the Rockettes. Well, come on down to Motel 5, and kill two partridges in one pear tree. You see, we've been receiving goods on a purely cash basis from some entrepreneurial spirits out there who like to keep a low profile, so we've got rooms packed to the ceiling with all kinds of great stuff in the original packaging and priced to go. So just check in, get all your shopping done, and treat yourself to a long winter's nap all in the same place. Motel 5. We'll leave the seat up for you.

DON'T THROW THROW PILLOWS

While the answer to What Women Need is perfectly clear to women, it has been a bedeviling mystery to men ever since the first guy dragged home the wrong wildebeest: "I said *small*. Does this look small to you, turtle brain?"

Men pretty much settle for whatever's easy and stick with it to avoid confusion. Women know exactly what they want and spend half their harried lives trying to train us to know what it is. I'm still in training, but as a public service I'll pass on a couple of tips.

For one, it's very important to remember that women need a lot more of certain things than we do. It's a law of nature, and fighting it is like being irritated by gravity: you won't change a thing, and it'll still be pulling you down. Among the things a woman needs more of are: time in the bathroom, candles, information about the neighbors' personal lives, things made of gold, silk and wicker, unguents, time to express her feelings, and pillows.

Among the things men need more of are: televised sports.

Today we'll concentrate on pillows. Men need one pillow, unless they've got a rolled-up sweater, which works fine and also satisfies man's need for multi-purpose objects. Men need things like clock-radios, reversible belts, and combination lug-wrench/wire-stripper/pewter engravers. This simplifies their lives because they have fewer things to break and lose. It also satisfies the need to impress their male friends: "See, you just flip this release gnurl and the flush-bracket toggles over into the flange nidget and you've got a gander bit. Neat, huh?"

For reasons still hidden in the genetic code, men need only one pillow and women need legions. If your mate is like mine, she needs several big, oversized pillows with lacey things around the edges, platoons of middle-sized pillows to prop up on the larger pillows, and squadrons of little throw pillows to prop up on them. This way she can render a queen-sized bed virtually impenetrable. And if you take even the smallest pillow, she will know. If you move a pillow to, God forbid, *use* it for something, then suddenly remember you're not supposed to actually *use* pillows and furtively put it back, she will know and will interrogate you. So you're better off just telling her that you were temporarily insane and moved a pillow and put it back before you came to your senses (do NOT tell her you grabbed it to smack something crawling up the wall—brrrr).

If you want to score some brownie points, surprise her one morning by making up the bed while she's in the shower. She'll love it. First, make up the bed, carefully smoothing out any wads or wrinkles larger than a toddler. Then try to remember exactly how she arranges the pillows and arrange them as artistically as you can. Stand back, cock your head, try to see in your mind's eye how she does it, and keep tweaking until you get it exactly right.

She'll get a huge kick out of this, because you won't even be close. No matter how hard you try, your artistic arrangement of pillows will look like sandbags holding back the levee. This will make her laugh and say you're sweet and precious and hug you while wearing the towel, and one thing might lead to another.

Finally, an important word about throw pillows: don't. Throw pillows are meant to be propped, stacked, displayed and arranged, but never thrown. Come to think of it, you can do just about anything with a throw pillow *except* throw it. Take my word for it.

O COME ALL YE AMBIVALENT

Christmas, to plagiarize a master, is the best of times and the worst of times, as many of us watch the season approach with a mixture of joy and dread. I don't even know what sugarplums are, but there was a time when they danced joyfully in my head. Now I wonder if they're a good source of fiber. Only those who leave carrots for the reindeer with wide-eyed excitement have unambiguous feelings about the season. Make no mistake, a sweet rendition of "O Little Town of Bethlehem" can still swell my heart; but a brain-dead clerk who gets me humming "O Little Clown of Bloomingdales" can swell the veins in my neck.

Christmas is not simply an excuse to go shopping, of course: It's a mandate. Thus women tend to enjoy the season more than men, most of whom would rather be clubbed with a gift set of Old Spice. If men could start their long winter's nap around the First Day of Christmas and regain consciousness just in time for the Rose Bowl, I think many would opt into the program. The whole business is just too complicated for most of us. Men tend to think that if they get a gift for everyone living under their roof, they've done their job, whereas women have lists as intricate as anything Homeland Security has compiled. It would never have occurred to me, for example, to give a gaily-wrapped cluster of goodies to all of our kids' teachers, even if I could gaily wrap—which I can't, lacking the gene. I can make a complete mess of a perfectly rectangular box, while my mother could wrap a live moose and make it look like it came from Macy's.

I once did a show for a Death Industry group— funeral directors, monument makers, casket dealers—and the weather was appropriately gloomy and funereal. I asked why they always had their annual conference in January, and an embalmer, who bore a chilling resemblance to Lurch, said it's because they're always in a good mood in January. "The holidays," he said in a hushed, sepulchral tone, "are very good for us." Brrrr.

It's no wonder, when you think about it. Given the sheer number of parties and rivers of good cheer consumed, it's pretty much inevitable that scores of pickled revelers will end up completely embalmed, often taking teetotalers with them, alas. Ho Ho Homocides tend to spike, too, of course: "He gave me a Cuisinart and his ex-wife a diamond bracelet, Your Honor. I didn't have a choice."

It's no mystery to me why there are more suicides during the holidays. One frigid December night I stood outside a store holding enough packages to give a reindeer a hernia and feeling my bone marrow slowly crystallize while I waited for my wife to bring the car around. She had chosen a rendezvous spot ten feet from where a robotic Salvation Army volunteer rang his little bell with the painful regularity of the devil's own jackhammer. I couldn't move or my wife wouldn't find me, and the bell was giving me violent tendencies and an unattractive tic. By the time my mild-mannered beloved battled her way through the Grinch swarm in the parking garage, she was ready to broadside an elf and I was asking passersby to please hit me in the temple with a tire iron to relieve my suffering.

Okay, I didn't actually ask, but I wanted to. Which is why we're dialing back our participation in the frenzy this year. All I want for Christmas is my two front teeth unbared and off the asphalt. And for you to have a very Merry Christmas.

COOL TACTICS

During the middle of the debilitating heat wave this summer, I emerged from my cool basement office to pick up the mail and found my wife standing three feet from a floor fan with her feet splayed and holding up the front of her skirt. Her eyes were closed in ecstasy as she luxuriated in the breeze ruffling her undercarriage. After a moment, she slowly opened her eyes, saw me enjoying the tableau, and in a breathy, contented voice said, "To air is human."

There's something about oppressively hot

weather that unleashes both our animal instincts and our creativity for combating it. For example, our wonder dog Kiko's instincts lead her to sprawl on the tile in front of the toilet, where she's not only in the coolest place in the house, but is in easy reach of the humans who frequently visit that particular corner and can't resist scratching her when she presents her belly.

Dogs aren't shy when it comes to seeking relief. A friend sent me a very funny photo: someone has obviously just poured a four-foot-long pile of cubes from an ice chest, and a boxer bulldog is stretched out in the middle of it in Superman flying position. Ahh.

We're friends with a couple who pride themselves on being Stealth Hippies. They dress conservatively to maintain their professional images while gleefully violating as many mainstream mores as they can get away with. So I wasn't surprised when they told me their favorite heat-beating tactic: they keep non-laxative suppositories in the freezer and use them as directed several times a day. They told me this while wearing cool, smug expressions. I had no follow-up questions.

My strategy for keeping cool is to take regular cool showers and not bother to get dressed until legal concerns arise.

When we moved to Kentucky, everyone assured us that the horrendously cold, wet winter was an anomaly and that we were going to LOVE springtime in Louisville. So you can well imagine how disappointed I was to have missed spring entirely because I was out of town that Thursday. From my perspective we segued abruptly from Deep Freeze to Biblical Flooding to Endless Lethal Heat Wave. I don't remember many breaks when we could leave the house without fear of freezing, drowning, or suffering heat stroke. Sorry, Mr. Limbaugh, but you won't convince me that global warming is a liberal conspiracy any more than you'll persuade me that privileged schoolteachers are at the root of the worldwide economic crisis. As I write this, it's 103 with a heat index of 110. I've got a towel on my leather chair so I won't stick to it because I'm wearing only my wedding ring.

I should point out that we have a fine central air conditioning system. But neither of us enjoys shivering in icy rooms, and of course we'd rather suffer hyperthermia than pay an exorbitant electric bill. We also simply love electric fans, which I just realized makes us Fan Fans. In fact, we're Fantastic Fan Fans, as I have a collection of wonderful old Eskimos, Polar Clubs, GE's, etc., which are a joy to look at, provide a delicious breeze, and have a sound that—for me, anyway—triggers time travel. Nothing transports me back to a simpler, more carefree time than the soothing ker-fladdle, ker-fladdle, ker-fladdle of a fan with a cast iron base and a wiggly-wire cage. I think a video of one could be as popular as the famous crackling fireplace (please make royalty checks payable to me, thanks).

My absolute favorite heat-beater photo is of an amply-proportioned woman in a tube top holding a hamburger in one hand, fries in the other, and sucking on the straw of her drink, which is doing double duty wedged into her cleavage. Judging from her husband's mullet and scarcity of teeth, he wasn't attracted by her refinement as much as by her practical problem-solving skills. I wouldn't be surprised if she had a popsicle secretly nestled in a crease somewhere.

HONOLULU, CITY OF CONCRETE

I've just returned from our beautiful 50th state, Hawaii, which richly deserves all the superlatives—it's the most laid-back state, the balmiest, and by far the most difficult to reach by car. That last one probably occurred to me because on the flight over I shared the last five rows of the plane with a tour group from the Institute for Evil Adolescents, who made the five-hour flight from L.A. seem like only thirty.

To help us keep our minds off the long flight (a baby was born just after we took off and was complaining in complete sentences when we landed), the airline showed a "Wonders of Hawaii" video that included a preview of a colorful Hawaiian variety show with leggy dancers and bowling-pin jugglers and magicians, the like of which you can't see anywhere but in Hawaii. Unless you count Reno, Atlantic City, Las Vegas, Lake Tahoe, Laughlin, Biloxi, Miami, and every cruise ship on earth.

After we saw clips of snorkeling and surfing and kayaking and hula dancing and pigging out at luaus, the same video was repeated; so two hours into the flight I was pretty much burned out on the whole Hawaiian experience and ready to go home. Then I remembered something my very wise old grandmother once told me: "If you can't enjoy a trip to Hawaii," she said in her sweet Southern drawl, "you ought to be drug outside and beat with a razor-strop." So, not wanting to be flogged at 37,000 feet, I tried to clean up my attitude.

I learned my first Hawaiian word from a pretty flight attendant who came down the aisle with a plastic bag collecting empty cups and napkins. Every couple of steps she would say "*Mahalo*," which means "Trash?".

Shortly after I reached late middle age, we landed in Honolulu. The beautiful tropical island of Oahu is divided into two very distinct sections: the beautiful tropical island part, and Honolulu, which loosely translates to "City of Concrete Overpasses."

On the way to the hotel, my cab driver told me he was from Manila, and I said, "Ah, where all the envelopes come from," and he looked at me in the rearview mirror exactly as if I had said, "I have iguanas growing in my armpits."

Making my plans months before, I had requested a room with a view. The reservations person told me they had just had a cancellation and, for no extra charge, she could get me a room overlooking the Kalawanahini, so of course I immediately grabbed it. For those of you unfamiliar with the islands, "Kalawanahini" means "Beige Air Conditioning Unit."

I went to a luau and learned a lot. For example, a traditional dish called *poi* got its name from the sound you make when you spit it out behind a palm tree. To give you an idea of how it tastes, when they found the Donner Party there were two cases of uneaten poi in one of the wagons. It's similar to petroleum jelly, but without the flavor.

I also had to pass on the *pupu* platter in adherence to my policy of not eating anything with the word *pupu* in it. You'll never hear me say, "Is the *pupu* fresh?"

I ate and drank lots of great stuff, though. I was lounging on the beach having a mai tai when I heard somebody behind me say "Mahalo" and instinctively looked to see if I'd dropped a candy wrapper. Then another person said "aloha," and I thought, Wow, I understand a lot of this language: luau, hula, aloha, mahalo. It's such a convenient language, because the alphabet has only eight letters and three of them are 'L.' Ukelele. Lei. Honolulu. Mahalo, mahalo vurry much. It also occurred to me that if you get enough sun, you can take home a special Hawaiian memory, "Melanoma."

I put on some sunscreen and ordered another mai tai.

PITTSBURGH (NUR)—The movie rating NC-17 has triggered a lawsuit by a man who saw it printed next to PG-13, thought it was a football score and attempted suicide. A spokesman said the man thought North Carolina had beaten Pennsylvania-Gorman 17-13, a larger point-spread than he had bet, prompting him to slash his ankles because one of his wrists was in a cast. An industry spokesman said that even more movie ratings are being considered, among them NM-12, or No Morons Who Act Like They're 12 admitted, and NJ-30, or No Jerks who say, "Watch This" every 30 seconds admitted.

HOLLYWOOD (NUR)—This just in from Hollywood: As of 6 p.m. tonight, informed sources report that not a single celebrity has gone public this week with a heartwarming story of personal triumph over drug or alcohol addiction. One reliable source reported that at least two actors have decided to postpone their drug addictions for at least six months so the publication of their heartwarming stories of personal triumph will coincide with the release of their latest films.

In other news from Hollywood: after actor Steven Seagal's mother contradicted his claims that he was a CIA adviser trained by an aikido master in Japan, the star of the movie "Marked for Death" said his real mother has been kidnapped by KGB operatives who replaced her with a ninja clone from outer space. Several claims Seagal made on *Late Night with David Letterman* have been discredited, but Seagal said lies about him are being spread by an intergalactic emperor of evil whom he will destroy in a fight to the death as soon as his current publicity tour is completed.

SPRENGUE FEVER

    I'm gradually amassing a body of evidence that indicates rather strongly that—while my wife and I are best friends and much in love—we are of different species. For example, on the first really warm, sunny spring day this year, my beloved and I were on the front porch reveling in the sight of songbirds cavorting in the warm blue skies and buds bursting forth when she did a little jig and said, "I've got spring fever!"

I thought *Wow, that's why we're best friends.* We're on exactly the same frequency. I've got spring fever, too! I feel like throwing a Frisbee or a baseball, lying in clover watching the clouds scud by, drowning a few worms while watching the river amble along, or maybe hiking through the woods with my .22 and blasting away at some cans.

I put my arm around her and said, "Me, too! What do you want to do?"

She rubbed her hands together in delicious anticipation. "I want to pull everything out of the closets, get rid of everything we don't need, reorganize it all, and do some serious dusting and mopping!"

I tried to maintain my bright grin, but it deteriorated into the expression of someone at a tea party who knows the hostess emitted a noxious odor but must pretend she didn't.

"Really?" I said, trying to sound enthusiastic.

"Yeah! Wanta help me?"

"Um."

If a fever ever compels me to do some serious dusting and mopping, it'll be dengue, not spring. Or maybe typhoid, because I'll clearly be delirious. I'm typically male in that I lack the Scouring Gene. I confess that I don't honestly see the logic of maintaining a surgically-immaculate toilet bowl considering what we routinely put in it. On the other hand, I do prefer ours to the ones commonly found in biker bars.

My wife knew I didn't share her rapture at the thought of cleaning closets, and she let me off the hook, bless her. She knows her Y-chromosome Neanderthal has vastly different urges, and she's given up trying to understand them.

Case in point: we lived in L.A. for 30 years before moving to Louisville, and our neighborhood was teeming with squirrels whose playful gamboling provided endless hours of entertainment to the average observer. Not being average, I saw them as destroyers of Christmas lights and an endless source of savory protein. I can say with some authority that I was the only resident of that city of ten million who regularly had buddies over to play pool and eat squirrel gumbo. Happily, the critters are easily fooled by a peanut on a trip-wire, and it takes only five of them to make a great gumbo—four if you catch a porker who's let himself go.

I once made the mistake of hiding one in the freezer in an unmarked bag, planning to thaw it out when I had time to skin and dress it. My wife thought she'd found a forgotten pork loin, instead discovered something looking back at her, screamed, and unilaterally passed a new household law on the spot: nothing with eyeballs, tails and claws allowed in the freezer.

Okay, fine. She insisted that I thaw and skin the beast immediately. I complied, but managed to infuriate her all over again. How was I to know she'd be home from the dentist that fast? Admittedly, choosing the bathtub as my theatre of operations was not the best choice, but the garage was a SAUNA that day.

THE ALL-GAY ARMY

All the controversy about gays serving in the military just screamed for a parody of some kind, and I've performed this one solo as well as with Jamie. We also did it as a commercial parody on our audio CD, Extreme Channel Surfing.

(*We hear rousing military drum and bugle music in the background*)

BIG, MANLY ANNOUNCER VOICE:
"In the old Army, if you blew away a dozen guys they'd give you a *medal*. But if you *blew* just one, they'd give you the boot. Not in the new, all-gay army, where we're looking for a few good men with impeccable taste in home furnishings. Be all that you *can* be, with a bunch of guys who wouldn't have you any other way."

(*Sound effect: 30 guys marching*)

DRILL SERGEANT:
"Shoulders back and belly in! (left, yo' left)
We just want a few good men! (left, yo' left)
Here they come them new recruits! (left, yo' left)
Sweaty boys in leather boots! (left, yo' left)"

HALF A DOZEN SOLDIERS:
"Here we come all young and green!
Big and strong and just eighteen!
Grab your t-shirt, grab your pants!
Who needs girls to have a dance!?"

DRILL SERGEANT:
"Hup-two-three-four, SING OUT LOUD NOW!"

SOLDIERS SING:
"*Somewhe-e-e-re over the ra-a-ainbow, wa-a-ay up hi-i-i-gh* . . . ."

ANNOUNCER:
The new, all-gay army. Strapping boys in leather boots, sleeping bags, and parachutes. It's not your father's army. See your recruiter today.

OUT

Instant Karma's Gonna Drown You

On the subject of Karma, it seems to me the population is divided into two camps: those like me who are strong believers in it, and soon-to-be believers who will inevitably get clobbered right between the eyes by a vengeful Karma.

For a solid year and a half after we bought our home in Louisville, my wife and I reported proudly that our wonderful 1930 house had "good bones," was in spectacular shape, and needed practically no work at all. Karma thought our "proud reporting" sounded suspiciously like "smug bragging" and decided that a Biblical deluge between the good bones would teach us a little humility. In a period of less than two weeks, our dishwasher sprang a leak, a trickle from our attic AC unit stained our bedroom ceiling, a small gusher flooded part of our basement, and a pipe burst, sending a waterfall cascading into our kitchen and demolishing an eight-by-eight-foot section of the ceiling.

Verily, we were chastened, stopped bragging, and frantically worked to get thumbs in all the dikes. We had to call a plumber to repair the burst pipe, but we fixed the other problems Ourselves. That's a reference to the fact that my wife will point thoughtfully at, say, a scraggly eyesore of tangled old shrubbery in the backyard and declare that it must be removed. "We could do that ourselves," she'll say, and of course Ourselves will trudge to the garage and sharpen up the ax.

Being handy is a blessing and a curse, of course. I save us a ton of money, but I burn a lot of brain cells trying to figure out how to do things the pros do without thinking. Another running joke is that I get the benefit of the Comedian's Compromise. If the drywall patch I've installed isn't exactly perfect, I just shrug and remind her that I'm a comedian, and that a drywall installer wouldn't even attempt to do what I do for a living. At least I gave his profession a shot, and chances are nobody will ever notice the miniscule irregularity beside the refrigerator. My wife is very forgiving and pretends to have blurred vision quite often, bless her heart.

Since I spend a surprising number of hours covered in paint, mud, sawdust, insulation, cement, drywall dust, spider webs, rust, mulch, and my own blood, it's probably not surprising that we have an official Splinter Removal Station. I'll yell, "Honey? Splinter!" and I'll hear her mumbling while she puts down what she's doing upstairs to meet me downstairs between the sink and the stove. She picks up the needle she keeps above the sink, sterilizes the point in a blue flame on the stove, clamps my affected digit in her left hand, and digs out the offending sliver. I could build a birdhouse with all the wood she's dug out of my hands.

The professional estimate of $3,000 to fix the leak in our basement was all the incentive Ourselves needed to give it a shot. The next time it rained heavily, I donned my grubbies and crawled through the mud under the deck looking for where the water was getting in. It wasn't rocket science. I moved a lot of dirt, strategically placed some plastic sheeting, spent $7 on concrete patch, and it hasn't leaked a drop since.

With that $2,993 we saved, we're definitely going to enjoy Ourselves.

MOTEL 666

I globe-trotted in my youth and have made my living as an entertainer for many years, so I've stayed in more cheap, scuzzy hotels than any non-fugitive on the planet—which makes me something of an authority. For example, did you know that every Motel 6 in the land accepts pets? Of course you didn't, but it's my job to know these things, being a contributor to *Condé Nast, Bottom Feeder Edition.*

I've stayed in a few rooms where the indigenous wildlife was large enough to be pet material, but let's leave that tour to Animal Planet. Once I checked into a fairly decent joint in Marrakech, and the innkeeper handed me my doorknob instead of a key. I had to carry it in my jeans pocket, which had an indecorous effect on my profile. Another time in Rabat I paid one dirham—about a quarter—to stay with six other guys in a room furnished only with hay. One of us had to stay in the "room" at all times to guard our belongings, because it didn't have a door, let alone a key.

Now I get to experience the other ludicrous extreme. I perform at a lot of corporate conferences, and often my palatial suite would more appropriately accommodate an oil sheik with four or five wives. I recently experienced the sublime and the ridiculous in one day. I had worked at a Ritz Carlton, where I know the client paid $482 for my room for one night because I peeked at the invoice. I enjoyed the robe, the shower gel, the Q-Tips, the loofah, the vibrating shower attachment, and the electric shoe buffer, because—well, come on. How many chances do you get? I had to stay an extra night to catch a flight to another gig, and since I had to pay for it, I got a room a mile away at the Emerald Inn for $38. There, the mattress was crunchy, the TV screen so small I couldn't read the scores on the bottom of Sports Center, and the amenity was a microscopic bar of soap I nearly lost in a flesh crevice. I saw the humor.

I had a gig in Vero Beach once and booked a room for two extra days at my own expense. I intended to use it as a retreat, hoping to finish a screenplay with a couple of uninterrupted days of work away from the distractions of home. I was stunned to find that a respectable national chain had a room for only $48 in a very good location, so I booked it before they noticed their mistake.

The first indication that it might not be a

mistake was when my cab pulled up and I saw the marquee: "Welcome, Nat'l Assn of Miniature Pinschers." Hm. As I checked in, I heard the distant "yip! yip!" of a dozen conventioneers. I asked for a room far from the doggy action, so the helpful clerk put me at the very rear of the hotel. Outside my window was a packed parking lot, and 30 yards beyond that I saw railroad tracks.

I unpacked and lay on the bed for a quick nap before starting work. I had just drifted off when I was jolted awake by the "DING-DING-DING-DING-DING-DING!" of the train warning signal going off at the intersection I hadn't noticed 70 yards from my door. This triggered a "yip-yip-yip-yip-yip-yip!" response from the agitated attendees, and a few seconds later an Amtrak train thundered by with a wall-shaking "WWAAAAWWWW!" This set off about 50 car alarms just outside my room, and the "WeeeUP! WeeeUP! BAwwBAwwBAww!" sent the Pinschers soaring into the next octave of annoyance, "YOWP-YOWP-YOWP-YOWP-YOWP!"

I didn't finish my screenplay on that trip. But I got an idea for another one.

MOTEL 5—"Animal Passion"

"Hi, I'm Tom Bidet for Motel 5, the absolute cheapest accommodations you can find this side of a freeway overpass. Over the years, we've found there are a lot of you fun couples out there who have a lot more animal passion than you do cash, so we figured out a way to let your libidos pay off. Just tell us you want to participate in our Pay-As-You-Play program, check into our special room with overhead two-way mirrors, we'll videotape the evening's main event, and you don't pay a thing. That's right, you have fun in a free motel room, and all you give up is worldwide rights to the videotape in perpetuity. And if you sign the contract without getting some stuffy lawyer involved, we'll even throw in a copy of the tape as our way of saying *Thank you.* So slide on in to The Best Little Roadhouse for exCESSes, Motel 5. We'll leave the seat up for you."

TEHRAN (NUR)—Iranian President Mahmoud Ahmadinejad has ordered government and cultural bodies to use modified Persian words to replace foreign words that have crept into the language, so "pizzas" will now be called "elastic loaves," "skateboards" will be called "wheels of Satan," and "Cheetos" will become "decadent orange food substitutes."

MOTEL 5—"Strong Convictions"

"Hi, I'm Tom Bidet for Motel 5, the cheapest accommodations you can find this side of a jail cell, and with much more convenient exits. In fact, if you've recently been a long-term guest of the state, what better way to ease back into society than by staying at Motel 5, which offers many of the inconveniences and Spartan surroundings you've grown accustomed to. In some of our earthier urban locations, we even feature 24-hour armed guards and actual bars on the windows, so you can wake up to the warm, nostalgic feeling of a total lock-down. And we don't like to brag, but a couple of former inmates have told us the chipped beef on toast in our cafe is exactly like the stuff they used to make them eat at the legendary Folsum Prison. So if you're a person of strong former convictions, come serve a little time with us. Motel 5. We'll leave the seat up for you."

BURY ME 'NEATH THE SPAGHETTI MONSTER

I was driving through rural Kentucky recently and was shocked by the number of roadside crosses marking the sites of traffic fatalities. Always crosses, never anything else. I was saddened and then annoyed, because according to the anecdotal evidence along the nation's byways, Christians are by far the worst drivers in America.

That raised my hackles because I was raised a Methodist and we're all great drivers, much better than Catholics or those distracted Presbyterians checking their Google Maps for the way to their predestinations. And those NASCAR-worshipping Baptists—Lord, don't get me started. Of course, many of the crosses no doubt mark a place where a godless drunk sent church-going innocents to their reward, so a cross doesn't necessarily represent the spiritual leanings of the culpable party. But after mulling it over, I finally came to the conclusion that when it comes to marking highway deaths, the other religions are obviously under-reporting. I kept my eyes peeled on the way to Paducah and didn't see a single Buddha Shakyamuni statue or Shinto shrine beside the road. I'm not familiar with their attitudes toward vehicular fatalities, but maybe a devotee of those faiths would be embarrassed to admit that a family member hit a bridge abutment, so a shrine would be a humiliating reminder.

True, the Shinto and Buddhist folk aren't heavily represented in Kentucky. But there's a significant Jewish population where I live in Louisville, and I have YET to see a Star of David beside the road. What are they telling us? That they don't make mistakes? Come on. The Jews produce an outlandish percentage of geniuses in entertainment, writing, mathematics—Streisand, Bellow, Einstein, etc. Could it be that they're also better than the rest of us at taking hairpin curves while under the influence? Or is it that they just prefer not to advertise where a Chosen One lost control and became one with a sycamore? I suspect the latter.

A devoted Muslim doesn't drink, so that

would tend to drive the fatality rate down for that group. But I know for sure that they text while driving, because I've been in some pretty harrowing cab rides with followers of Islam at the wheel. The foot on the gas pedal is often as leaden as the facial expression in the rear-view mirror checking Smart Phone messages. Of course, Muslims have legitimate excuses for not leaving a memorial where a believer has been martyred by a fishtailing Kenworth. For one thing, they're rarely unanimous about anything and so far haven't been able to agree on a symbol. But even if they had one, within hours of its roadside appearance, a patriotic local would take it out with a 12-gauge or just plow through it with his F-150 because it's not the old rugged symbol his mama 'nem sing about every Sunday.

An atheist symbol would of course get desecrated even faster than a Muslim one. But while the non-believers can't agree on a single symbol, their attempts have been pretty amusing. The Darwin fish with feet gets a smile from all but the hardest-shelled theists because it's clever but a clear slap at Christians. A crimson "A" has been suggested, the atomic symbol is used on military tombstones denoting "No Religion," and the Invisible Pink Unicorn camp (I'm not making this up) has a web site where you can buy IPU pins and t-shirts. My favorite, however, is the Flying Spaghetti Monster, which of course symbolizes something that doesn't exist. I somehow just can't imagine anyone wanting a wide-eyed, red wiggly thing marking where his last text abruptly ended.

WILL YOU BE MINE IF I SHOW IMPROVEMENT?

If there are any guys out there who actually look forward to Valentine's Day, I suspect they own stock in companies that sell candy, greeting cards, or flowers. The folks over at See's and FTD are thrilled for good reason, but you won't catch me fattening up their bottom lines. My wife doesn't allow me to buy her candy for fear of fattening the lines of her bottom, and I can never remember which flowers make her sinuses explode like sea monkeys.

So I'm off one hook and firmly impaled on another, i.e., the necessity to be creative on a day when most guys take care of their obligations in two five-minute surgical strikes on the florist and drugstore. Of course, V-Day blindsides us less than two months after Christmas, and my wife's birthday falls between them, so that stretch can be rather stressful for a guy like me trying to keep his marriage healthy.

What makes it particularly challenging, of course, is that we Martians often don't have a clue what makes Venusians happy. If you thought, for example, that a Self-Lowering Toilet Seat would ignite smoldering animal desire in a Venusian, you'd be doing some typically masculine, Left-Brain, knuckle-headed thinking. And while Chanel #5 is an obscenely over-priced, totally impractical gift, it's much more likely to trigger warm expressions of gratitude than a garlic press, just FYI. Or a stainless-steel colander. Even top of the line. Seriously.

Generally speaking, my wife and I tend to celebrate our gender-based differences, but they can occasionally cause a teensy bit of friction. She doesn't understand, for example, how I can easily go a solid week without buffing, dusting ,or scouring anything and not feel a void in my life. On the other hand, I can't fathom why a sock left on the floor of a closet for less than a week should cause her consternation when not even a CIA spy satellite can detect it.

Our differences have actually inspired some pretty creative projects. For example, I was actually working on a design for that Self-Lowering Toilet Seat when I Googled it and saw that there are about a dozen patents pending for such a device. Not that I forget to lower the seat more than ten or twelve times a week, but she still thinks it could save her a few trillion brain cells over the life of the seat. My own in-house study has revealed that my forgetfulness has a dramatic negative impact on her romantic friskiness.

There are definitely areas of my life that need improving, and I'm the first to recognize it. Okay, second, truth be told. I have been known to take an occasional break from my typical tireless and frenetic pace of doing household chores, for example, and nothing animates her Inner Life Coach quicker than the sight of me slouching on the couch with a beer in my hand watching a game on TV, which recently inspired her to suggest that maybe I needed to get outside for some fresh air. Of course, 27-degree air is "fresh" to some, and "debilitating" to others, like me.

Still, the mortar of a good marriage is compromise and sacrifice; so the day after her suggestion, I watched a bass fishing tournament on ESPN. We loaded the boat, I never left the couch, and I had to admit she was right—I felt a lot better. So much better that I checked the listings, and the next day I went deep-sea fishing off Aruba. I think the fresh air is doing wonders for me.

MISSISSIPPI DAWNING

NOTE FROM THE AUTHOR: I'm a professional comedian, and I was born and raised in Mississippi. Coincidentally, my upcoming novel is about a Mississippi boy who grows up to be a professional comedian. It's not an autobiography by any stretch—I have two brothers and no sisters, for example—but I thought you might enjoy a sneak peek at a chapter.

"Do I have to wear socks?"

"Don't be silly, Mason, it's church."

"It's not regular church, it's just Tuesday night."

"Revivals are regular church, and we're visiting, and you're not going in there looking like the Wild Man of Borneo. Here."

She handed him a heavy pressure cooker to wrestle onto a low shelf, and continued putting away the lunch dishes that had air-dried in the rack.

"Rita Gail's not wearing socks."

She closed her eyes and sighed. "Girls don't have to wear socks, Mason, and you're not going to be the only thirteen-year-old boy in the church not wearing socks, and we're not going to talk about this, so don't start."

"Why do girls get—"

"I said don't start. I don't know why girls

don't have to wear socks, they just don't. It's a law I didn't make up."

He decided to remind her that longstanding cultural traditions were dissolving in Mississippi.

"We're supposed to be equal."

"Fine. When she has to wear pantyhose, you can wear pantyhose, too, how's that?"

"Can I stand by the windows on the side?"

"You know they put extra chairs for the women over there. Quit belly-achin', Mason, they'll have the ceiling fans going. Bring a fan."

"It makes you hotter if you have to work a fan."

She slammed a drawer shut and whirled, thrusting a spatula inches from his nose. "You know what makes you even hotter than that? When your Daddy burns your stubborn butt up with his belt, and that's what I'm going to get him to do if you don't get your mule head ready to walk out the door in three minutes! Do you understand me, Mason Randall Davis?"

"Yes, ma'am. I'll wear the tan ones, they're thinner."

The sound of his full name made the tops of his ears burn as he slunk down the hall to his bedroom. He'd made her angry, and he really hadn't meant to. But intentional or not, he'd made a mess that needed cleaning up. If Mama was mad at him, the conversation in the car would be as strained and heavy as a bag full of cottonmouths, and would no doubt remind Daddy of something else Mr. Smart Butt needed to be chewed out about while he was at it. And he could forget about a butterscotch sundae at Ray's after the service. He had spit in his chili, as his Uncle Shug would say, creating a clear and present danger to his peaceful evening. He had to lighten the mood, and began to strategize as he pulled on his socks and penny loafers.

He came back into the kitchen and put away some coffee cups without being asked. Then he laid out the bait with a light touch, while deftly reminding her what a hard-working, generous young man he was.

"Can we go to Ray's after church? I've got some mowing money, so I can buy mine and Rita Gail's."

Unless she was madder than he'd calculated, she'd think about it for a moment, then say it depends on how long the service goes.

She put some spoons in a drawer, thought about it a moment, and said, "It depends on how long the service goes."

Mason knew he should feel guilty for setting the trap, but Brother Gartner himself had said Christians used the talents God gave them and sinners did not. He remembered the point very clearly, because on the drive home that Sunday, he'd asked his parents about people whose talents were things like making whisky and writing dirty books. Hank and Nell had quickly looked out their respective car windows in the front seat to avoid eye contact, and he'd seen a faint hint of the telltale pinkish splotches on the back of his mother's neck as she tried not to laugh. Rita Gail—who at fifteen disapproved of practically every breath her brother took—had snorted, "God, Mason," and folded her arms and scooted as far away from him as she could get, which was a fair distance in the back seat of the 1957 Chevrolet Bel Air. After a moment's reflection, his mother had cleared her throat and said people like that were sinners because they were using their God-given talents for the Devil's work and not the Lord's.

Mason couldn't imagine that making people laugh could be the Devil's work, although Mitchell Wayne Fulton told jokes in the boys' restroom that would probably qualify. But he honestly didn't think the Lord would punish him for making his mother laugh, even if it caused her a little physical discomfort. Making a joyful noise, even if wasn't exactly unto the Lord, had to be a good thing.

Mason reached up and straightened a stack of saucers in the cabinet so his comment would sound off-hand as he set the hook: "Lord, I hope Sonny Tillman don't rededicate his life again."

"Now Mason, that's—" She disguised a giggle as a snorting cough and turned to straighten the perfectly straight salt and pepper shakers on the back of the stove while she fought to regain normal breathing. She kept her back to him and bit down hard on her lower lip, pushing the laugh deep into her stomach. Mason knew she would have changed the subject had she been able to speak, so he had successfully executed Step One: rendering her helpless. He had worked her like a matador, leading her into the open, creating a diversion, setting her up, and then blindsiding her. He knew in his heart that it wasn't right, but—as if some unseen power was manipulating him—he just couldn't help himself.

"If Sonny gets the Holy Ghost we could be there 'til breakfast."

"Mason?!" she sputtered. "I mean it! Th-that's not Christian." Her shoulders quaked, and rosy splotches started flowering around the base of her neck. She took a deep breath, trying to collect herself. "The Lord speaks to different people in different ways."

Mason couldn't believe it. There it was—an unexpected gift that he immediately recognized as a fatal tactical error. Sweet Nell Davis, bless her unsuspecting heart, never learned to avoid the easy set-up, thus providing Mason early training for his future career. Nell's God-fearing, humanity-loving, Sunday-school-teaching brain would release an innocent utterance out into the world like a wide-eyed, unsuspecting baby bunny, only to have Mason pounce on it with startling, deadly agility. In this instance, it never occurred to Nell that since Sonny had a pronounced lisp, it would be very ill-advised to use the word "speaks" when alluding to him. While it floated like a bunny in mid hop, Mason hit it like a timber rattler: "Do you think He thpeakth like thith tho Thonny can understhtand what He'sth thaying?"

Her face turned radish, her legs buckled, and a series of sob-like respiratory explosions shook her upper body as she tried to keep the laughs from coming to full bloom. Closing her eyes tight, she aimed a stiff finger at Mason, dagger-like, warning him not to say another word. "Don't!" she ordered. He obeyed, because he didn't think his actions thus far were punishable, and this was no time to press his luck. She bent over and huffed, her face stretched into a painful-looking skeleton's grin. Her knees snapped together and she covered her abdomen with both hands and baby-stepped as quickly as she could down the hall toward the bathroom. She banged on the locked door with urgency.

"Hank! Open it! Now! Hank! Now!"

She had already pulled her skirt up and was struggling with her pantyhose snaps when the door opened and she hopped through the door, her knees together.

"My Lord, Nell, what in the—?"

"Ohhh! Just move, Hank!"

The whap! of the toilet lid and the *buh-duh-bap* of the seat hitting the porcelain echoed down the hall. Rita Gail rushed from her room wearing one shoe and carrying the other.

"Mama! What's wrong?!"

"Just shut the door, Rita Gail!" said Hank. "Mother's fine! Go on!"

Through the door, Rita Gail could hear Nell sputtering, snuffling, laughing and crying at the same time. She could hear her father stifling giggles as her mother sat on the toilet, quaking with suppressed laughter. She heard her father whisper, "What did he say?"

Rita Gail's eyes narrowed and her jaw jutted forward. She strode down the hall with her arms crossed and found Mason flipping through a *Reader's Digest* as if he had seen and heard nothing.

"Did you do that?"

"Did I do what?"

"Don't play innocent, Mason. Did you make her pee her pants again?"

"We were just talking and she got tickled, you know how she is."

Rita Gail had long, straight, copper-colored hair, and every inch of her fair skin was crowded with freckles, some so close together that they touched and formed little cinnamon splotches. Nobody knew why the Irish or Scottish blood had suddenly flowered so conspicuously in the

Davis line, but there she was, and a feisty streak came with the coloring. When she was upset her face and neck glowed red, and she was very clearly, radiantly upset.

"You can't just do that, Mason, it's not right!"

"How do I know what's going to make her pee her pants?"

"You know very well, and it's not funny!"

"She thought it was."

"Don't be a smart alec, Mason, you know what I mean."

"Daddy makes her laugh every day."

"He doesn't make her pee her pants."

"How do you know? They wouldn't tell us if he did."

"He can't get to her like you can. You've got a—" She stopped, unable to come up with a suitably disparaging term. "You've got this thing, and you know it."

He did know it, but what was it? What was the word Rita Gail couldn't bring herself to say? What did he have? A power? A gift? A curse? He knew that he had a talent for making people laugh; but, for the first time, the notion that he had a special power stirred his imagination. He'd never thought of it like that. It was just something he could do naturally, like when Ricky Baxter threw his shoulder out of joint and wrapped his arm around his head like it was rubber. That wasn't a power, either, just a thing he could do that other people couldn't.

He'd always taken it for granted because his father was always the funniest grown-up in whatever group they found themselves in. At family get-togethers his father could tell stories and have all his aunts and uncles rocking with laughter. He could play Aunt Flo like a fiddle, making her howl and screech and titter until she glistened and glowed and wiped her eyes. Flo's husband, Uncle Lester, couldn't tell a funny story for all the corn in the county. If he tried to tell a joke he'd heard at the feed store, he'd tell the punch line first and then try to work his way back and get hopelessly lost and flustered and finally just shake his head and grin and flap his hands like he was shooing gnats and give up. Mason's Daddy could make a funny story out of nailing tarpaper to the wood shed, and it would just roll out like he'd planned every word.

Teasing each other and making silly comments was part of their everyday lives, and Mason remembered how odd it was to him when he first learned that some households were devoid of humor. He went home from school once with his buddy Leon Taylor, and the frigid silences that Leon's parents dragged around the house made him very uncomfortable. His attempts at mild humor had been met with dull stares or even thinly-disguised hostility. Leon had a huge mutt named Booger, and when Mason commented that Booger looked like he could eat a whole pig in one sitting, Leon's father had scowled at him and said, "He better not be chasin' no pigs." At dinner, they said only what had to be said, like "Pass the beans," and not in a particularly pleasant tone. By the time he left, he knew exactly why Leon cherished Mason's company and followed him around at school. Leon's house was a humor-free zone. The more time he spent in other peoples' homes, the more he realized his was special.

One Sunday when Mason was nine, they were at a pot-luck dinner at the church, and he had stuffed himself with deviled eggs and fried chicken and ambrosia and pecan pie and didn't feel like running around with the other kids. He lay in the slight shade of a wispy mimosa tree, chewing on grass and watching ants file across the roots. Every time he heard a burst of laughter, he'd glance over to where the folding tables were lined up on the lawn and see a group of men laughing at something his father had just said.

After awhile Nell ambled over and sat beside Mason and asked him if he was feeling all right. He said he was fine and quickly changed the subject so he wouldn't have to confess his gluttony.

"How did Daddy get to be so funny?"

She waved at a fly, then picked up a twig and twirled it for a moment. She looked a little troubled, and Mason wondered if he'd said something wrong. "He might not want me telling you this, but the fact is that your Daddy had to endure a lot of hurt when he was a boy. I think when he finally got out of that situation and was able to fend for himself and be his own person, he just decided to make up for lost time and have as much fun as he could. Look over there. There's two solid acres where those men could be standing, and they're all within six feet of your daddy. He's just a natural at making people laugh." She smirked. "He found out pretty early that it was a good way to get girls, too."

"Is that why he got you?"

She smiled and nodded slowly, focusing on a distant time. Mason could see she was peeking in on herself twenty years ago. "I dated some better-looking boys, some more ambitious boys, some boys that everybody knew would end up rich. But not one of them could make me laugh like your daddy, and I'd rather laugh every day than have all the fancy cars and diamonds in the world."

"So you married him because he was funny?"

A little chuckling hum came from her throat and she took his chin in her hand. "I married your daddy because I was in love with him. I fell in love with him because he treated me like a queen and could make me laugh my head off."

At the time, Mason couldn't imagine ever wanting to treat a girl like a queen. But he had to admit he loved turning over Vonnie Kay O'Connell's tickle-box. She was a year older than him and a Catholic, so they could never get married. But she'd squint her eyes and purse her lips in anticipation of laughing every time Mason came near her at school; and when she laughed, her whole face would crinkle up like a newborn kitten's and her cheeks would glow like a fever. And it didn't take much to set her off. If they saw hefty Mrs. Colmer sitting on the edge of a table in the cafeteria, all he'd have to say is, "Boy, I feel sorry for that table," and Vonnie Kay would cut loose a machine gun giggle.

Now, with his mother in the bathroom trying to regain control of her bodily functions, he felt the scorching, accusing eye of his big sister and knew she was plotting to somehow make him atone for his sin on the ride to the church. She might even break their pact and relate the unfortunate BB gun incident of the previous week that cost one of the evil Lanham twins a 45 record. He decided he had nothing to lose. "I made some mowing money this week doing the Herrings and the McMillan's," he told Rita Gail. "I told Mama I'd buy us both a treat if we went to Ray's."

Rita Gail threw her hair forward and expertly pulled it into a sheaf. Her mother sometimes tried to get her to "wear it pretty," but Rita Gail was an athlete and practical and didn't wear her hair for the boys yet and didn't like it in her face.

"Well," she said, unwilling to acknowledge his offer. She couldn't be nice to him when she was scheming to crush his spirit, particularly while her mother was still suffering from the painful bladder episode he had cold-bloodedly triggered. It would have felt to her like a betrayal. She made a ponytail and snapped a rubber bolo band around it. "Don't get your hopes up," she said. "If they sing every verse of 'Just As I Am' during The Invitation, we won't even get to go."

"Yeah, and you can say 'Goodbye Ray's' if the Holy Thpirit thpeaks to Thonny Tillman."

Rita Gail's stoic resolve instantly crumbled as she covered her mouth and burst into muffled giggles, stage-whispering "Mason!" between snickers. "You're horrible!" she said, and slapped him on the arm.

"He'sth already rededicated hith life to Jethuth theven or eight times, tho I think Thonny's got more lives than a Thia-meethe cat."

She shut her mouth and eyes as tightly as she could, sniggering through her nose, and clamped her palms over her ears. Her face flushed strawberry red, with spokes of white around her mouth and eyes where she puckered her skin bloodless. When she had enough breath to make a noise, she started humming, "La la laaaa la, la la laaaa la," and patting her ears so she couldn't hear him. Then she made the mistake of looking at Mason, who had assumed the prayerful, splay-legged position Sonny would take as he stood at the altar and rededicated his life to Jesus for the eighth time in two years. She bent over and sprinted down the hall to her room and slammed the door behind her and Hank yelled "Stop slamming doors!" from the bathroom. Mason noticed how much Rita Gail looked like their mother when she ran, and his whole body tingled with power.

After Nell and Rita Gail had gotten into the car, Hank led Mason to the rear bumper and gripped his shoulder and put a finger in his face. The smile in his eyes told Mason that he wasn't angry, but his body language said that he wanted him to take his words very seriously. "You know what you did, and you know I can't whip you for it," he said. "But I don't want any emergencies on the way to church, or I swear I'll pull the car over and take off my belt, do you understand?"

Mason gave him his Innocent Imp expression and nodded. "Yessir."

"Good. I mean it, Mason."

His father slapped him playfully but firmly on the behind and they got in. They managed to stay on neutral subjects on the twenty-minute ride, but Hank had to raise a warning finger once when Mason pronounced "Methodist" with a skillfully subtle lisp. "Yessir," he said quickly, carefully pronouncing the esses, as Rita Gail and Nell simultaneously looked out their windows.

The parking lot of the Jackson Creek Methodist Church was full when they arrived, and a man in a blue short-sleeved shirt darkened by sweat stains waved them onto the adjoining softball field. He told Hank he'd be all right if he stayed away from left field, which got mushy after a rain.

A steady trickle of people filed into the church in the waning summer light. Hank and Nell greeted a few friends from their own church, and Hank got chuckles from a couple of the men. Mason had to admit it was kind of refreshing going to church and not seeing the same old faces. He recognized the basketball coach from their rival high school in Pascagoula. He shook hands with an electrician who worked at the paper ill, then shook the startlingly soft, childlike hand of Mr. Coe, who owned a shoe store. He shook the hard hands of shipyard pipe-welders, and the knobby one of Mr. Walters, who had lost two fingers, ironically, on Number Two paper machine out at the mill. Mason knew at least half a dozen men who had lost fingers or parts of fingers at the mill, and one who lost his arm up to his elbow in the pulpwood chipper.

Rita Gail saw her friend Ellie and they tarried on the edge of the crowd, chattering and sneaking peeks at a couple of teenage boys who were inspecting a moth they had caught. Mason said Hey to his friend Luther, who played first base for Burnham Freight Line, the best

Little League team in Bayou Heron. Mason was a fleet-footed outfielder for Brumfield's Department Store. They agreed that the coach of Dixon's Hardware had falsified his son Rupert's birth certificate so he could play an extra year. Rupert was the only kid in the league who had to shave before every game. Luther was saying he thought Rupert might be adopted when he looked past Mason and his face flushed and he stumbled over his words. Mason turned to see Tammy Tolbert whirling through the crowd, all a-bubble, saying Hey to everybody, her ponytail and breasts bouncing athletically, her cheerleader teeth the brightest point in the gathering dusk. She flitted through the crowd like a luminescent hummingbird among a flock of mud-colored sparrows. Tammy was sixteen, and the object of many an adolescent's desire. Mason figured she'd be a movie star when she grew up. He glanced over at Rita Gail and Ellie and knew they were exchanging snide comments about Tammy because she was beautiful and bouncy and curvaceous and they weren't. Girls were meaner than boys, in his estimation. He'd heard gossipy girls described as "catty," which was an apt description—they were secretive and haughty and sharp-clawed. Mason heard his name and looked up to see his father gesturing that it was time to go in. He told Luther he'd see him later, and walked into the church with his family.

Mason was pleased to see that the pews were almost full, and many of the younger men were already standing. Word had gotten out, the Reverend Billy Clyde Pemberton was packing them in, and there was no place they could all sit together. Mason knew he couldn't take a seat if there was a single lady standing, so he hung in the back with his father as Nell and Rita Gail found a spot together in the fourth pew from the front. He looked up to see that Tammy was going to walk right past him, and positioned himself to soak in a gulping, full-frontal dose of her radiant aura. She gave him a quick smile, then stopped right beside him, looking for a place to sit. She raised an arm to tuck a hank of hair behind her ear, and the smooth half moon of flesh between her armpit and her right breast suddenly winked at him within touching distance. Mason was shifting his stance to get a better look when the pianist started banging out "Bringing in the Sheaves." A bucktoothed man near the pulpit raised a burgundy hymnal and shouted out the page number and started belting out the song, and the congregation followed along. Mason didn't have a songbook but didn't need one, having sung the song an average of once a week since he was seven—"Sowing in the morning, sowing seeds of kindness, Sowing in the noontide and the dewy eve." He sang as he watched Tammy slide into a seat a couple of pews away, then looked up to find that his father was watching him watch Tammy. Hank cocked an inquisitive eyebrow at him, and Mason grinned and shrugged—his dad would be the last person to admonish him for looking at a pretty girl. Hank gave him a mock frown of disapproval and motioned for Mason to stand against the wall. Mason found a spot behind a man in a wheelchair, while his father found a place on the other side of the sanctuary. Perfect, thought Mason. He could probably lean on the wheelchair handles, he could see everything, and he wouldn't feel his parents' eyes on the back of his neck through the whole service. If he leaned forward slightly, he could even see the smooth crease between Tammy's thighs where she hooked her left knee over her right. He suddenly felt he was being watched and saw his mother near the front, twisting in her seat and trying to will him to look at her. When their eyes locked, he half-smiled and wiggled his fingers at her. She raised her eyebrows and crooked her head, meaning, "Behave yourself," and he nodded.

Two rattling old ceiling fans were moving a little air, but it was still stifling in the sturdy heart-pine building. Practically every lady in the church held a cardboard fan with a flat wooden handle and fluttered it at her face. When Mason was a little boy, his mother would occupy him during the service by letting him look at the fans and their pictures of churches and scenes from the Bible. He remembered one of Jesus stepping out of the cave after the rock had been rolled away and He arose from the dead. He had read about caves in the Tom Sawyer stories but never actually seen one. Caves were practically non-existent in marshy, swampy southern Mississippi, and the one Jesus walked out of had always fascinated him. He used to wonder what it would be like inside, and wished he could go in and look around.

Moths and June bugs whizzed and flapped drunkenly against the screens of the large windows on either side of the sanctuary, and a couple of flying insects had gotten inside and were buzzing around the ceiling. Mason saw a dead June bug caught in a spider web at the base of one of the ceiling fans. He was reminded of the legendary Sunday night when one landed on Miss Polly Beckham's neck in the middle of Brother Gartner's sermon. Miss Polly was a rather frail and nervous spinster, easily overwrought and allergic to an astonishing variety of flora and fauna. When the insect clamped onto her neck with its scratchy little legs, she bucked in her pew like a scalded mule and unleashed a blood-curdling shriek that triggered a chain reaction of screams from the ladies and girls in attendance. Mason was only seven at the time, but could remember very clearly the unearthly caterwauling that sent goose-bumps rippling across every square inch of his body. For a few unforgettable moments, utter chaos reigned in the sanctuary. Bernard Wilkes had been sitting behind Miss Polly, saw the critter latch onto her neck, and instinctively shot his hand out to catch the bug, using his other hand to steady Miss Polly's head. So when the entire congregation whipped around to find the source of the commotion, their first impression was that Bernard—a mild-mannered, 50-year-old father of four and treasurer of the church—had gone temporarily insane and was choking Miss Polly from behind. As he grappled for the insect, saying, "June bug! June bug!" many assumed he was addressing Miss Polly, confounding even those with the most vivid imaginations, who couldn't fathom why in the name of Heaven the ordinarily bashful Bernard Wilkes would be strangling Miss Polly in church while calling her pet names, particularly with his horrified wife Raynelle's expansive backside right beside him occupying a third of the pew. The incident ranked among the more surreal Mason—or anybody else at the First Methodist Church of Bayou Heron—had ever witnessed.

"*Bringing in the sheaves, bringing in the sheaves, We shall come rejoicing, bringing in the sheaves.*"

Even as he was making a joyful noise, Mason rejoiced at the appearance of a couple of late arrivals—Sonny Tillman and his mother, Myeerah, who looked like a mattress in a floral dress. Another unexpected gift, he thought, as sofa-like Myeerah roughly steered red-faced Sonny down the aisle and bulled her way into a pew, causing a chain reaction as the line of seated congregants scooted, wiggled, and inched, caterpillar-like, until a man on the other end extricated himself and stood against the wall, leaning on his cane. Mason looked up front and was pleased to see that his mother and Rita Gail were unaware that Sonny was in the building. If Sonny made his presence known that night, a surprise appearance would be much more effective.

Myeerah was obviously on a mission, and Mason rejoiced and was exceedingly glad. Judging by the contrite look on Sonny's face and the large square of gauze taped to the nape of his red neck, Sonny had once again been tempted by the Devil, led into wickedness, and caught red-handed by his All-Seeing mother, who was there to oversee yet another soul-cleansing of her backsliding son. Mason could only guess what Sonny's infraction might have been; but since they'd celebrated the Fourth of July only a week before and at least one injury had apparently resulted, chances were good that pyrotechnics were involved. Sonny loved blowing things up. He lived for the holidays when fireworks stands sprung up in vacant lots along Highway 90 like seasonal red-white-and-blue plywood flowers. In the long lulls between the munitions-heavy celebrations, Sonny saved every penny he earned to buy cherry bombs, Black Cats, Roman candles, M-80's, bottle-rockets, and what were still called "nigger-chasers" in 1964 Mississippi. Sonny was the only person Mason knew who had the restraint, patience, and dedication to save fireworks for occasions not traditionally associated with explosions, like Thanksgiving and funerals. Back in February, Mason had witnessed one of Sonny's crueler stunts on George Washington's Birthday, the first school holiday after New Year's. He and Lionel Roberts, his partner in evil, tied a string of Black Cat firecrackers to the tail of Mrs. Kimball's cat Toodie and sent the terrified creature careening through bushes and up pecan trees in a horrifying display of wanton wickedness.

"*Sowing in the sunshine, sowing in the shadows, fearing neither clouds nor winter's chilling breeze.*"

Lionel had threatened Mason with a beating if he tattled on them. Mason knew it wasn't an empty threat—Lionel enjoyed beating up smaller, weaker kids—so he kept quiet.

As Sonny sat beside his mother looking like the poster boy for adolescent misery, it was obvious that he hadn't been so lucky this time. Mason watched him pick at his bandage. Mrs. Tillman slapped his arm to make him stop, and she seemed to take the opportunity to hit him harder than necessary. Sonny had no doubt had at least one whipping already, but still had much penance to do. Tonight was just another step toward full atonement.

"*Bringing in the sheaves, bringing in the sheaves, We shall come rejoicing, bringing in the sheaves.*"

As the congregation sang the final chorus, Reverend Billy Clyde Pemberton strode down the center aisle from the rear, smiling and shaking hands as he shouted "Praise Jesus!" and "Sing it strong!" between the lines of the hymn, his slicked-back red hair gleaming with a Brylcreem luster. With his red hair, and in his yellow short-sleeved shirt and a red-striped tie that reached to the top of his belly, he looked like God's own banty rooster ricocheting between the pews, raising a worn Bible above his head when he shouted. As if it had been choreographed in Hollywood, the bucktoothed song leader melted into the congregation and Billy Clyde reached the pulpit just in time to belt out the last line of the song with the congregation, leading them to hold the last three notes, creating a fresh and dramatic climax to a well-worn hymn, and Mason felt the congregation collectively suppressing the urge to applaud wildly. Brother Pemberton had revived the crowd before he'd even opened his mouth to preach.

"A-men hallelujah, praise the Lord and bless you all for coming out tonight!" he shouted through a luminescent grin. "And I know! I know it's hot! I see those fans a-flutterin' and I know I'm gonna be a-wringin' wet before this night is over, and that's all right, 'cause Lord knows I could stand to lose a few pounds!" The crowd tittered. "But I say praise God that y'all knew it was gonna be hot and y'all came out here anyways, 'cause somebody's gonna be a lot hotter than us tonight, children! Oh, yeah! This ain't hot! Oh, no! 'Cause we gonna be immersin' ourselves in the cool, refreshin', thirst-quenchin', life-givin' Word of God and baskin' in the beautiful breeze of the Holy Spirit filling our hearts with gladness, so you know who's gonna be sweatin' it out, don't you? That's right, the Devil's gonna be a-squirmin' on his old evil throne tonight, children, 'cause we gonna make it hot for old Satan tonight, let me tell you! Ha! The Devil hates the Truth and the Light, y'all, and we gonna give him a double dose of it tonight!"

"Amen!" said some of the older men.

"He's gonna look up from that fiery pit and say, 'What in the world is goin' on at the Jackson Creek Methodist Church!? They settin' off a atom bomb of Christian Love right smack in the middle of my evil empire!' Ha! Yes, sir! We gonna make it so hot for him that before this night's over, old Satan's gonna wish he had a 'lectric fan and a nice cold Barq's Root Beer to cool off that forked tongue of his, ain't he?!"

More Amens! punctuated the general laughter, and Mason found himself grinning, transfixed by Billy Clyde Pemberton's performance. He glanced over and saw that his dad was hooting and slapping his knee, Mrs. Tillman's cinderblock face was softening into a smile, and even Sonny looked like he might find a way out of the brimstone.

"He's already feelin' the heat, folks, 'cause nothin' makes the Devil happier than an empty church, you see." He raised his arms to take in the standing-room-only crowd, smiling rather devilishly. "I think y'all have got his knickers in a bunch tonight!"

Amens and belly laughs.

"Aw, no, this ain't to his likin' a-tall. He ain't used to hearin' that beautiful anthem on a Tuesday night, so he got confused, ya see, kinda discombobulated. Well, you just listen up, Mr. Satan, 'cause I got a bulletin for you: tonight, Jackson Creek Methodist Church is Devil Discombobulation Central!"

The congregation erupted in belly laughs, foot-stomping, and hymnal slapping. Mason slammed his palms on the wheelchair handles and apologized with a gesture when the old man turned to look at him. A few folks got carried away and clapped their hands a few of times before they remembered where they were, and Leonard Watts even whistled like the Bayou Heron Mudcats had just scored a touchdown. Nobody minded, because Mason could see that everybody wanted to cheer like they were at a ball game. He wondered why the Holiness churches were allowed to carry on like that, with their electric guitars and drums and Lord knows what-all right there in the sanctuary, shouting and clapping and speaking in tongues and doing all sorts of fun things the Methodists didn't allow in the House of the Lord. He remembered the night a big tent had been erected in a cow pasture near his grandparents' home up in the country for a Holiness revival. They wailed and sang and pounded on their drums, making noise that could be heard for half a mile, and Mason's Papaw Turner was not amused. "Would you listen to that racket? Howlin' like a buncha alley cats gettin' their tails twisted!"

Mamaw Turner tried to get him to show a little religious tolerance. "Now, Willis, that's just their way of worshippin' the Lord."

Papaw snorted. "Well, do they think He's deaf?" and Mason had to leave the room to laugh.

Billy Clyde Pemberton wiped his face with his handkerchief and stuffed it into his back pocket.

"A lot of y'all sang that wonderful old hymn from your heart, like you are primed and ready to rejoice in the love of Jesus." He paused and cocked an impish eyebrow at the crowd. "I have to say, though, that some of you was singing like you'd say the pledge of allegiance to the flag." He said the next line robotically, with no inflection at all. "Just kinda lettin' the words tumble out like you've done a thousand times before, out of your mouth and not from your heart."

The crowd chuckled and he grinned. "I'll be honest with you, folks. Some of you was singin' like your favorite dog just got hit by a pulpwood truck."

He paused for the laugh, and Mason studied him as he timed his next zinger. Billy Clyde hung his head as if in mourning, his face drooped into a comically sad-sack expression, and he sang tunelessly, cheerlessly, as if on the verge of tears: "Bringin' in the sheaves, bringin' in the sheaves." He paused as the laughter swelled, echoed, rolled past the altar and then receded like a wave. He let the silence hang for a second, two, three. Then, in the same miserable voice, he moaned: "We shall come rejoicing . . . " and there was no need to finish since no one would have heard him over the tidal roar. The pews shook with laughter, people threw back their heads and slapped their thighs, and Mason saw Tammy's smooth, perfect legs uncross as she bent forward in a paroxysm of giggles, her hands covering her angelic mouth, her cheeks flushed, the hair on the nape of her neck damp with her sweet sweat.

Just as the laugh was dwindling to silence, Billy Clyde raised an eyebrow and cocked his head at somebody in the second row, pointing out an alleged rote-singer, which unleashed another crashing wave—and he hadn't said a word. He'd revved the laughter to another eruption with a gesture, an attitude, a subtle physical movement that wouldn't get a laugh on its own; but, when tied to the image he'd just planted in everyone's minds, triggered that most wondrous of gut reactions. Billy Clyde Pemberton was a virtuoso, and played the crowd like a musical instrument, knowing exactly when to raise his voice and when to take it down, when to jump on the next line and when to pause, when to smile and when to flash a mock frown, when to flail his arms and when to stand still. Mason marveled at his artistry, and his heart was thrilled by his performance.

Billy Clyde had The Gift, and years of perfecting it had given him the power to move people in a magical way. He strutted, he shouted, he boomed out belly laughs of his own, he looked up and talked directly to God like He was sitting in the rafters. He heckled Satan mercilessly, fearlessly, hilariously, and banished him from church and the county and the state. He said funny things and he said things funny, and he sprinkled the sermon with anecdotes and asides that kept the congregation smiling and nodding and shaking their heads and saying Amen. He told them a spiritual person needn't be a boring person, that Christians can laugh and have as much fun as the drinking, swearing, adulterating sinners, but without the ravaging effects on their loved ones and their mortal bodies and the eternal damnation of their souls. He told Biblical stories that brought Jesus to life as a flesh and blood man as strong as a pipe-welder, as tough as an oil-rig roustabout, as accustomed to sweat as a millwright on a 90-ton paper machine. To Mason, the way he talked made you feel like he was talking just to you, and that Jesus is alive, and real, and good, and He loves you so much that He wants you to leave your sinful ways behind and give your life to Him and walk in the ways of righteousness so you can all meet again in the Sweet By and By on That Beautiful Shore. In forty magical minutes, Billy Clyde Pemberton had that congregation rocking and swaying and laughing and praying and singing and shouting and sweating and crying, and when The Invitation came, a respectable trickle of emotionally-wrung-out New True Believers strode to the altar to wipe their tears and shake Billy Clyde's hand or hug his sweaty neck and be saved or rededicate their lives to Jesus. The preacher went down the line, holding each one's hand as he closed his eyes and prayed heavenward. Finally, seven people stood at the altar as the congregation sang the third verse of "Just As I Am," but Sonny Tillman held tight to the top of the pew in front of him, reluctant to admit that he had succumbed to the Devil's temptations once again. Myeerah sang stoically, occasionally aiming a hypodermic glance at her wayward son, but aware that the final choice had to be his own.

Sonny was obviously struggling with the demons in his coarse little heart as the next-to-last verse began: *"Just as I am, poor, wretched, blind; Sight, rich-es, heal-ing of the mind."*

Billy Clyde shouted over the singing, "Someone is holding onto that pew in front of them with white knuckles!" and Mason saw Sonny pull his hands from the top of the bench as if from a hot stove.

"Yea, all I nee-ed in Thee-e-e-e to find, O Lamb of God, I come! I come!"

"That's Jesus Christ the Redeemer talking to you, sinner! You know the Lord saw what you done, don't you?" and the Lord and Myeerah glared holes in Sonny's burning, quivering, crew-cut criminal head.

"Oh, He saw you, all right! That's the bad news! But the wonderful news is that He still loves you, and He'll forgive you if you just ask him! You're just one of his lambs that's gone astray, and he wants you back in the fold!"

"Just as I am—Thou wilt receive, Wilt welcome, pardon, cleanse, relieve."

"Just come down right now and He'll lift that burden right off your heavy heart!" Sonny's shoulders quaked, and Mason saw his lower lip quivering, fluttering, flapping, stretching into a sob.

"Be-e-cause Thy promise I believe, O Lamb of God, I come! I come!"

As the last note was sung and the hymnals were folded shut, Billy Clyde raised his hand and said, "Please be seated," and everybody who had a seat did—except Sonny.

As everyone else in the pews settled into their seats, Sonny—woeful, wretched Sonny—stayed on his feet, wracked with remorse and shame. Scheming, deceitful Sonny, who had heard that Mr. Delancey was going after king mackerel south of Petit Bois Island on Saturday, and happened by when he saw him hosing down his boat late that afternoon. Lying, conspiring Sonny, who told Mr. Delancey he was doing a science project involving fertilizers and needed a bucket of fish guts. Sinful, misguided Sonny, who fabricated an ingenious stink-bomb from a milk carton, fish guts, and four cherry bombs. Diabolic, backsliding Sonny, who placed the bomb on the tea-table inside the playhouse of the evil Lanham twins, and fashioned a fuse that would give him and Lionel time to hide in the overgrown fence-row fifty yards away and watch as the interior of the playhouse was instantly and deafeningly painted with a fresh coat of fish viscera. Miscalculating, unlucky Sonny, who didn't count on the limp fuse doubling over and igniting itself where it entered the carton. Star-crossed, short-sighted Sonny, who couldn't follow Lionel through the play-sized window before the bomb detonated, blistering his entire anterior half with a salty, deep-sea slurry and burying a sharp chunk of mackerel cartilage in the nape of his neck and a fin bone in his right thigh. Conspicuously criminal Sonny, who staggered, howling, bleeding, and temporarily deaf, out of the playhouse, after the equivalent of a half a stick of dynamite alerted Mrs. Lanham, Mrs. Kimball, Mr. Bracken, Mrs. Miles, Mr. Carpenter, and a black man fixing Mr. Bracken's roof that something had gone horribly wrong and a child was injured and needed to be tended to immediately. Indisputably, undeniably, aromatically guilty Sonny, who was literally covered in evidence, pieces of which would have to be removed in the emergency room.

Penitent Sonny stood there trembling, tears streaming down his red cheeks, and Billy Clyde looked across the congregation at him, smiled beatifically, and stretched out his arms, calling him home. "It ain't no use to fight it when the Holy Ghost has got aholt of you, son. Come on down and let Jesus take that heavy load off of your heart. Come on, now."

Everyone seated between Sonny and the altar slowly turned to see who the preacher was addressing, and Mason watched with excited anticipation and a needlepoint of exquisite dread as Nell and Rita Gail simultaneously turned. Blood rushed up Nell's neck like mercury up a thermometer, and she snorted, gagged, and whipped her head back around and stared at her knees, shaking with unexploded giggles. Rita Gail spewed a burning nose-laugh, whimpered audibly and sank in her seat until Mason could see only the top of her head gently bobbing up and down above the pew, like a fishing cork being worried by a bluegill. They were both struggling, shaking, and several people around them looked over with concern, as if they were sharing some kind of seizure.

Sonny pushed his way past Myeerah's tree-trunk knees and trudged toward the altar with a slight limp. Billy Clyde and several of the older men said, "Amen!" and "Praise Jesus!" and Mason couldn't have agreed more but was too young to give it voice. He didn't have to look across the sanctuary at his father to know he was glaring at him. The laser stare that burned his left ear was so powerful that it caused it to itch and he rubbed it with his hand. His mother and sister were scrunched together tightly, their heads bowed, no doubt praying that Sonny wouldn't be allowed to utter a syllable. But the Lord works in mysterious ways, and on this night the Almighty bestowed upon Mason his first-ever "call-back"—which Mason would learn years later is the comedian's term for a laugh that blooms from a seed planted earlier.

Billy Clyde motioned for Sonny to approach him, and he shook his hand and then put his hands on his shoulders. "What's your first name, son?"

Quietly: "Thunny."

Mason heard simultaneous mewling sounds, and several people glanced at Rita Gail and Nell, hunched completely over now, hiding their faces in their hands on their knees and shaking.

"Thunny?" said Billy Clyde.

Nell wheezed painfully and Rita Gail coughed and keened, clearly nearing the limits of containment.

Mason heard Sonny whispering an explanation to Brother Pemberton, one he'd no doubt been forced to use often, something like, "No, Thonny, like the Thunny Thide of the Thtreet."

"Ohhh, Sonny, I'm sorry, Sonny. Well, I can see that the Lord is speaking to you tonight, Sonny. Do you feel him in your heart?"

"Yeth thir."

Nell decisively grabbed the top of the pew in front of her, jerked herself vertical and lurched past the row of knees to the aisle as Rita Gail followed, practically pressing her face into her mother's back. Both of their faces were pinched into pained scowls as they gritted their teeth and bit the insides of their mouths.

"I'm going to pray for you in a minute, Sonny, but if you're going to accept Jesus Christ as your Savior, you're going to have talk to God every single day yourself, you know."

"Yeth thir."

Nell had made it to the aisle and was walking toward the rear of the church with modified baby steps, pressing her hand over her face. Using her mother as a shield, Rita Gail also covered her face as they edged toward the rear exit like a single, semi-blind four-legged beast. People glanced over, but didn't want to stare at someone obviously in some kind of physical distress.

"And what do you want to say to the Lord tonight, Sonny?"

Sonny took a deep breath, sniffed, and said loudly and wetly, "I want to thay I'm thorry that I've thinned!" and Nell's left knee buckled, her body convulsed, and she spewed a spray of spittle onto the carpet. Rita Gail stage-whispered, "Keep going, Mama!"

"I'm tho asthamed of mythelf, *snort!* becauth I've thinned and fallen thshort, *sniff!* and I want to athk Jethuth for forgiveneth of my thinsth *snerk!*"

Even over the scattered chorus of Amen! Hallelujah! and Praise the Lord! the violent WHAPPITY BAP! BAP! of the swinging door in the back as it flung violently open and recoiled caused several people to jump and turn to see what caused it, but Nell and Rita Gail were gone. Mason would learn later that Nell made it to the row of camellias on the side of the sanctuary, where she flailed into the bushes and pulled her pantyhose down and leaned on the wooden siding of the church and found relief.

Mason watched them burst out the door, then locked eyes with his father. Hank was trying his best to glare menacingly, but Mason could see the forbidden chuckle pushing hard on the underside of his scowl. Mason didn't know what his consequences might be. He assumed that a butterscotch sundae at Ray's was out of the question for that particular night, but didn't know if his father was contemplating giving him a whipping. He decided that if he were to be punished, he'd take it like a man, because he felt in his heart that what he'd done wasn't a sin in God's eyes. And, regardless of the consequences, it was worth it. Hadn't Jesus died on the cross for what he believed? Hadn't men died in battle fighting for freedom? Enduring five or six licks with his daddy's belt would be nothing compared to those sacrifices. He'd grit his teeth and squeeze the edge of the chest of drawers and take his licks without fear or complaint, because he believed in what he was doing. He'd been following his heart and practicing his calling. For Mason had a life-changing epiphany that night: God had made him a natural-born comedian, and Billy Clyde Pemberton had brought that vague notion into crystal-clear focus and inspired him in ways the good reverend hadn't intended. Like Billy Clyde, Mason had The Gift. If he could use it for Good, why not go for a little Power and Glory as well?

DONKEY DELICACIES AND MAN-EATING TRAINS

They say nothing broadens your worldview like traveling, and after enjoying the decidedly decadent delicacies across France and Italy for 17 days, my wife and I are feeling extremely broad. We've eaten so much stinky cheese and baguettes that our French has improved considerably. To speak French properly, you have to purse your lips and crinkle your nose as if trying to determine if the cheese is ripened to perfection or flush-worthy. The line can be maddeningly fine.

Happily, along with our fleshy parts, our minds have also expanded. Here's just a tiny sampling of the culturally enriching tidbits we picked up on the Continent:

- It's so difficult to find good donkey sausage in our community that you'll be delighted to know that it's ubiquitous in France. Which won't do you any good if your spouse refuses to allow it in the same car with her.
- On any given day, there are roughly the same number of Chinese in the Louvre as in Kowloon.
- If it's just been too darned long since you swooned in the presence of the dried tongue and vocal chords of a saint, you can find relief in a cathedral in northern Italy.

We spent a lot of time in our nifty little rental car. Some of our friends think we're insane for driving in foreign countries, but we love making up our itinerary as we go, and picnicking where we choose. And of course it's vastly fulfilling to take potty breaks—discreetly and legally, of course—in the most spectacular settings imaginable. In fact, I was much more discreet than the local guys, who just pull to the shoulder, turn their backs to traffic and fire at will. I deferred to Miss Manners and always found a bush.

A few years ago in Ireland, I thrilled at the challenge of shifting a four-on-the-floor with my left hand while driving on the wrong side of the road. When the 10-ton lorries zoomed toward us on narrow roads, I got a little tense, but only ruined four pairs of shorts. And since we don't sky dive or drag race anymore, we've found that a scenic way to get the same adrenaline rush is to drive across the Alps with impatient Italians in Ferraris trying to kill us. Tailgating is a popular sport in Italy. High-speed vehicular sodomy is a way of life. Of course, it would be imprudent to show your annoyance by flashing an obscene gesture, because that numskull pressuring your sphincter could be the hot-headed son of the local Don. I'd rather dine on the Fish of the Day than sleep with it.

My other near-death experience occurred on the Metro, the famous Parisian subway system, when the very first train we boarded tried to eat me. I carried cameras, guidebooks, and baguettes in a little backpack. When we surged forward with the crowd, a busker with a violin caused a horrendous bottleneck in the doorway. I managed to get my body onto the car behind my wife, but my backpack didn't make it. The doors closed on it, and I was stuck like a bug on a pin, helpless to do anything, while the alarm buzzer howled at me in French: LeWAHWN! LeWAHWN! LeWAHWN! A couple of beefy guys managed to pry the door open and extricate me, but of course I was mortified and felt like the stereotypical Ugly AND Stupid American. My wife found it vastly amusing but pretended not to. She couldn't help herself when two hours later I walked past a bicycle chained to a post and the handlebar caught my backpack strap, jerking me to the ground as hilariously as a Stooge.

With the incredible food and sights keeping

her amazed—and various modes of transportation assaulting me and keeping her entertained—my wife had a wonderfully fulfilling trip. I did, too, but I'm thrilled to be home.

THE DECLINE OF WESTERN AIR RAGE

The FAA recently reported that the number of air rage incidents is declining, but they don't know why. Of course, it's easier to assess things that happen than things that don't: "Excuse us, sir, but we noticed that you didn't sucker punch a gate agent or defile a beverage cart. Could you explain why?"

Maybe the FAA meetings are helping: "Hi, I'm Bob, and I'm an airline employee abuser."

"Hi, Bob! What can we get you to drink?"

I did an extensive poll in my metropolitan area of all the frequent flyers living in my immediate home, and my data suggest that air rage incidents are declining because 1) monster portable electronic devices are now available, and 2) flying with morons eventually causes you to lose the feeling in your brain.

I am a typical business traveler (despite what my wife would have you believe), so I have enough frequent flyer miles to go to Neptune (I had just qualified for a weekend on Mir when it broke). In any case, I certainly qualify as a member of "the flying public," and in recent months, my own air rage incidents have declined dramatically, plummeting to roughly one homicidal rage per flight.

I don't report this to brag, but to use

my own experience as a typical passenger to explain the baffling statistic: I have finally been granted the serenity to accept the things I cannot change, and the wisdom to know that beating somebody to death with a laptop won't get you to Cleveland any faster.

For example, I used to get a tad irritable if I were napping when the person behind me raised his tray table to its full upright position at approximately the speed of sound. If it's never happened to you, imagine being kicked in the back by a mule wearing hushpuppies. Your first instinct is to grab the flotation device. Your second instinct is to grab a heavy, blunt object. But, being a reasonable person, you go with your third instinct, which is to bark a sarcastic remark over your shoulder like, "Could you slam that tray table into my back a little harder, please? I'm trying to nap, and it might knock me unconscious. Thanks so much!"

That was before I attained serenity. Now, I just sigh and try to go back to sleep, because trying to explain the physics involved to a person who thinks *your* seat is in fact *his* foot-rest/kickplate/handrail/drum pad is like trying to teach your cat to crochet. They'll both wonder why you're looking at *them* while you're doing your lip and tongue exercises.

I finally realized that these people are not to blame for their moronic behavior, because there's clearly something about airports that lowers the IQ of the average person. Maybe the jet fumes gum up an important brain function, or maybe it's the combined aromas of Danielle Steele "novels," mocha frappacino, and shoe polish.

Something's doing it. Otherwise, 67 average people wouldn't hear "Please remain seated until your row number is called," and simultaneously translate it into "Please grab your oversized bags, stampede to the doorway and clog it up so no one who actually complies with the gate agent's instructions can possibly claw through the scrum without starting a fist-fight. Thank you."

Now, I just smile benevolently, because I have achieved Enlightenment, and because I have a pair of artillery-resistant headphones that cover roughly half the surface of my head and make me look like a Russian cosmonaut from 1961. So when I've got my "Babbling Brook" tape cranked up to "Niagara," the passenger beside me could have Tourette's and a trombone and I'd never know it.

Thus my conclusion that air rage incidents are down because 1) Moronic behavior eventually dulls the victim's senses, and 2) Industrial-strength portable electronic devices help dull the morons. And if you folks at the FAA have any more questions, just ask—unless I'm wearing headphones and a sleep mask.

CINCINNATI (NUR)—In a riot-related case, a compromise has finally been reached after bitter fighting over the racial makeup of a jury. A spokesman said the defense and prosecution had finally agreed to a compromise: three jurors are black, three are white, two are off-white, two are pebble beige, one is antique white, and one is mocha creme.

TEHRAN (NUR)—A special report from Iran:

What are the Iranians really hiding? Long-range missiles capable of reaching Israel, or, as the ruling council claims, harmless machinery for a new facility called "Khomeni World, the Mother of all Theme Parks?" Sources say one of the rides, the Space Martyr, can hurl fun-seekers up to 300 miles.

LOS ANGELES (NUR)—More celebrities are risking millions in the high-stakes fragrance game. While Liz Taylor's "White Diamonds" and Cher's "Uninhibited" have been runaway successes, Martina Navritalova's "Jock Sweat" hasn't been doing well, and sales of Barbara Walters' "Wosebwossom" have been disappointingwy woe. The men are getting into the action, too, as Sylvester Stallone will soon introduce his new men's cologne, "Testostallone," which will sell for about $30 and come in two big brass round things.

SPAM AND EGGS

If I took advantage of all the Male Enhancement offers that clutter my Spam box, I'd soon look like a fireplug with fifty feet of hose. If I took advantage of a tiny fraction of the Cialis and Viagra offers, the hose would be pointing at the tenth floor like a howitzer.

The avalanche of such offers puzzled me, because I really don't visit web sites that suggest I have a burning desire "to make hot Russian babes scream." The mere thought disturbs and exhausts me, and makes me shudder to imagine the seething mob of vodka-fueled Ivans and Vladimirs I might antagonize in the process.

Then at a party I heard a klatch of women laughing about all the Viagra ads and offers to Enlarge their Manhood they were flooded with daily, and I felt much better. Apparently the sleaze-balls who claim they can transform cocktail weenies into bratwurst take the shotgun approach. If they've got your email, they're going to try to sell you the dream of genital grandeur whether you've got the required equipment or not.

They used to really annoy me, but now I just accept the wild claims as unsolicited entertainment. "Be the star of your neighborhood with your new love machine." Hm. Not likely. I know MY neighbors wouldn't be impressed, and the dinner invitations would no doubt drop off. Loved this one: "So hard you can break an egg." Wow. Would anyone really want to, even for "America's Got Talent"? I guess it would bring a Benihana-type excitement to breakfast, but a) I'd hope to find a more constructive use for the condition, and b) the logistics just don't appeal to me. I think if I demonstrated such a skill for my wife, she'd probably go with a bran muffin that morning. After reminding me where the cleaning supplies are.

I'd say that roughly 99% of the spam I get is comically misdirected. Right under a pitch for a Miracle Enlargement Pill, for example, I was asked if I've tried the "new Vaginal Mesh Patch." I haven't, and frankly wouldn't know where to start. Spackle came to mind, but for what?

I was chagrined to see that "Single Christians" in my area are looking for me. They're obviously not looking very hard, because I'm not exactly in Witness Protection. But if they're really looking for a thoroughly married man, then that's not very Christian of them. Apparently Black Singles Over 50 are also interested in finding me—Christian or pagan wasn't specified—but I'm afraid they're going to be very disappointed if they find me.

Awkward English gives away a lot of scammers. The instant I saw "Your pre-approved for a $5,000 loan," I knew I wouldn't be doing business with a financial professional who hasn't mastered basic contractions.

Even if I wanted to "Get Hight Quallity Pills Without Perscription!" I probably wouldn't trust my life to a pharmacist whose pitch read like a ransom note from a Somali pirate.

I found the come-on for Humongous Bouncing Boobies both eye-catching and amusing; but again, wrong target audience. I'm just not a fan. Mountainous breasts have always intimidated me, like I wouldn't be man enough to make them happy.

Today's offerings were particularly dramatic. Someone has allegedly "Run A Background Check!" on me, apparently to see if I'm actually qualified to start my "New Career in Law Enforcement!"

I can see I'm not even going to have time to order my "Amazing Genie Bra!" that eliminates rolls, wires, and adjusting straps. Glory. Humankind is saved.

I Take Thee and These

What is it about an impending wedding that drives women insane? Okay, not all women, but enough of them to shame the gender. I thought I was aware of the most common aberrant pre-nup behaviors—starvation diets, lavish spending for an outfit she'll wear once, hiring armed guards for ice sculptures—until I read an article about how plastic surgeons are making millions tweaking brides (and, alarmingly, their mothers!) so they'll look more like Barbie on the big day. Manicurists and hair stylists are still useful, of course; but if the procedure doesn't require anesthesia, it's apparently not sufficiently transformative for the modern bride. They're whacking and botoxing to beat the band and bowdlerize the blushing bride. They're even having botox parties for the bridesmaids! Hideous matching outfits aren't enough anymore. Now they must have hideous matching pouts—a garish school of ladyfish blowing champagne bubbles.

The irony, of course, is that presumably the victim—I mean groom, sorry—popped the question because he found the one woman on earth who's perfect for him in every way. And now that he's committed, her first official act is to make permanent alterations to the package he proposed to? Come on. To me, that's a rather egregious bait and switch, like a groom showing up at the church with a brand-new five-inch tarantula tattoo on his neck ("Bitchin' bachelor party, Brad!"). I married the cutest little leprechaun on earth and would have been horrified had I raised the veil to find a botoxed and basketball-boobed Barbie. Brrr.

I have to think a lot of guys would feel the same way. What if the guy really liked the original model and recoils at the options he didn't ask for? Maybe he loved her little tush just the way it was and doesn't like the rubbery squish-bag she had implanted. Maybe he rather enjoyed the natural pliancy and easy handling of the 34 B's, and isn't entirely comfortable scaling the taut new plastic twin peaks. And, of course, when he's bent and shriveled, creaking along on his aluminum walker, she'll be beside him, shuffling on wrinkled stalks, but with the dual dirigibles still plowing proudly ahead, holding up the rest of her sagging body like helium balloons. Seems to me he should at least have a say in how gracefully they're going to age together.

"Jason, do you take Sarah, and all the things that aren't quite Sarah, until death do you part, with the knowledge that some of her parts have a half-life of 400 years?"

"Well, gosh, I don't know. Is that botox going to wear off, or is she always going to look like she's about to say 'poot'?"

Seems to me if you're going to get a pre-nup tuck or implant foreign substances, you should at least clear it with the guy who's going to sleep with it for the foreseeable future. Of course, that leads to the first of a lifetime of fraught questions and marital Catch 22s. If he says No to the surgery, he's a controlling tyrant who doesn't let her make her own decisions. If he says Yes, he doesn't like her body and wants her to hack off chunks of it and pump up others so she'll be worthy of his devotion. Makes "Does this dress make my butt look big?" seem easy: "No, honey, bacon-burgers, Gargantuan Guzzles and never moving it made your butt look big."

Where will spiffing up for a wedding end? Liposuction for the 10-year-old ring-bearer? Laser fuzz-removal for the pre-teen flower girls? But I'm probably years behind, as usual. A Kardashian probably does that every time she's a bride.

*   *   *

And while we're on the subject of body augmentation, I thought this poem I wrote on the topic would give you a chuckle.

TIME FIGHTER

Bubble, bubble, boils and stubble,
Cheeks that sag and chins that double,
Creeping crow's feet, spider veins,
Cellulite gone unrestrained.

A tooth not quite like all the others,
A nose that could have been your mother's,
Crepe-y neck and liver spots,
Breasts like shriveled apricots.

Can nothing stem decay so foul?
The wilting lids, the flapping jowl?
The drooping buttocks, puckered eyes,
The corrugated knees and thighs.

But wait! Who comes to dam the flow,
Repulse the cruel, relentless foe!
Who dares to staunch the march of time?
To challenge nature's ugly crime?

It is I! your stalwart knight!
Who battles Time's unholy blight!
'Tis I alone can stop the clock!
For beauty is my trade and stock!

I give you, by my honor bound,
What Ponce de Leon never found!
You think I commit perjury?
Nay, Reconstructive surgery!

Augmenting this! and whacking off that!
Contouring mounds of hideous fat,
I'll tweak and lift and pinch and hone,
And lipo-suck you to the bone!

Collagen to smooth you out,
Implants, stitching, glue and grout!
A perfect smile I'll engineer,
With caps and porcelain veneer.

I'll tattoo eyelids, brows, and lips,
And fabricate a schoolgirl's hips,
I'll excise every imperfection,
With my brilliant vivisection!

Mother nature's met her match,
I'll nip and tuck and peel and patch
This lumpy bag of bone and grease,
Into a living masterpiece!

LONDON (NUR)—After witnessing superb performances during the World Cup quarter finals, the International Olympic Committee is considering making Injury Faking an Olympic sport. A spokesman said Olympic Whining is also being considered, and matches still tied after an extra period would be decided by penalty kicks to the player's groin. In related news, the American Association of Sports Fans has appealed to World Cup officials to modify the rules of soccer to make the game more appealing to Americans. Among the suggestions to increase scoring are widening the opening of the goal by about forty feet, and allowing each team six gang tackles before penalties are assessed.

ATLANTIC CITY (NUR)—Enraged when the city's casinos were shut down over the 4th of July due to a state budget crisis, angry gamblers today were given the opportunity to give the casinos the money they would have lost under a new "No Chips Left Behind" program.

Atlantic City's Under-Commissioner of Gaming, Luigi "The Shiv" Bonzelli, said the casino community was reaching out to disappointed gamers who might be forced to waste their paychecks on food or diapers. He said they could drop the cash into special troughs at the entrances to casinos, and in return would receive a coupon for a free French fry at select casinos in Reno.

Vowing that the gaming industry would never be caught unprepared again, Bonzelli announced the opening of an Emergency Gaming Range where gamblers could throw cash off an overpass into a dump truck, with a large payout if it went into a salt shaker. A reporter from *The Newark Star Ledger* observed that throwing cash into a salt shaker is impossible, and was the instant winner of a free deep-sea fishing trip with Mr. Bonzelli's associates.

THE DESIGNATED IRRITANT

I was at a dinner party at a friend's house recently where everyone in attendance either walked or rode a bike, which is another thing I love about our neighborhood. Ironically, the chat turned to travel, and among us we'd visited practically every interesting place on earth. My neighbors like to socialize locally, but they get around globally.

I have enough frequent flyer miles to go to Neptune, so I thought as a public service to my fellow globe-trottes I'd share a recent discovery that might make your next flight more tolerable (first, a quick one: if you don't allow for the change in air pressure when you open your little cup of yogurt, you might deplane looking like you've been in a food fight).

Today's startling revelation: The airlines put a Designated Irritant (DI) on every plane.

Now, before you get annoyed, be assured that it's for our own good, even the good of the country. You have to trust them on this and *relax* when you spot one. That baby wailing non-stop from Louisville to Dallas? Its diapers have been soaked in ice water. The woman whose gum-popping simulates sniper fire? She's on the payroll. Those drunken conventioneers yelling potty jokes all the way to Orlando? They're a team working the plane together.

I finally figured it out on a flight out of Chicago. The flight had been delayed six hours for the usual silly stuff—ice storms, tornado warnings, "dangerous" wind-shear conditions—so I was already steamed when we finally boarded. Then a woman apparently preparing for a Gucci-sponsored assault on Everest dragged onboard a pile of gear that took twenty minutes, two flight attendants, and a volunteer team of civilians to stuff into the overhead bins.

By the time we finally got to cruising altitude, I was livid. I slouched in a steaming funk behind my sleep mask, trying to lose consciousness while mentally working out the details of a class-action suit, when a piece of metal *RIPPED* off the plane, *THRUMMED* violently against the fuselage and jolted us twice more with a bone-jarring *THWACK! THWACK!* I tore off my mask and was clawing for my inflatable seat cushion when I saw the guy across the aisle *THWACK!* his deck of cards on the tray table once more for good luck. Then he started *SNAP!*ping the cards over one at a *SNAP!* time, in case anybody had the *SNAP!* mistaken impression that this was the first time he'd had these SNAP! babies in his hands.

Of course, our founding fathers set down the Right to Shuffle and Snap right after the one about bearing armor-piercing ammunition, so all I could do was grit my *THRRRRRRUPP!* teeth and picture the guy T*HWACK! THWACK! THWACK! THWACK!* roasting in hell, or at least finding out his daughter is living with a musician. Yeah, a musician who rebuilds Harleys in the kitchen, ha ha! Yeah, hee hee! And then his wife calls from Buenos Aires and tells him the $10,000 worth of liposuction worked so great she ran off with the pool boy and all their savings! HA!—and—

Then it hit me: I wasn't cursing the airline anymore. I was throwing hexes on a fellow pas-senger! I'd shifted my rage from a huge corporation to an obscure little dweeb playing solitaire! What a great scam! *THRRRRRRUPP!* The airline had worked me like play-dough! *THWACK! THWACK! THWACK!* I wasn't plotting against the airline anymore, I was plotting to spill my tomato juice on a deck of cards! I'd fallen for it!

Somehow, knowing the guy was just doing his job made it okay. A fellow working stiff, dedicated to protecting the airlines from frivolous lawsuits that would drive ticket prices sky high and flood the job market with unemployed flight attendants. I pushed back my sleep mask, gave him a sly, knowing smile, then a thumbs up. He pretended to be confused, even disturbed that I was looking at him like that. What a pro! Without a word, he got up from his seat and went to do his duty in another part of the plane. And I went to sleep to the distant *thrrrup* . . . *thwack thwack* of a dedicated DI doing his job.

THE NATIONAL SLEEP FOUNDATION

A poll by the National Sleep Foundation found that almost two-thirds of Americans are sleep deprived and fight to keep from napping at their jobs, while four-fifths of all adults surveyed said there's no way they could say they worked for the National Sleep Foundation with a straight face.

About seven-eighths said they would sleep for a week in cold meat sauce to get a job at the National Sleep Foundation, and eleven-sixteenths said they'd like to work in the Doze and Daydream Department.

A poll of the nearly three employees here at the Sarcasm Institute revealed that nearly half were amazed that the NSF even exists, and wondered if the funds were furtively appropriated when a majority of Congress had nodded off.

To find the answer, we went straight to the source and called the NSF. After about 20 rings, a croaky voice said, "Hello?" I said, "Is this the National Sleep Foundation?" and the voice said, "Yeah. Do you know what time it is?" I said I wasn't sure, but—

"It's 10:30 in the morning," he whispered hoarsely, "and I'm at work. Do I call you and wake you up when you're at work? Have a little respect," and he hung up.

I started to call James Walsh, the vice president of NSF I saw quoted in the paper, and tell him about his surly employee. Then it occurred to me that maybe the NFS is like Hollywood, where you sleep your way to the top. Walsh might be grooming this guy for something. The guy might have been faking sleep in case Walsh called to test him.

I tried another extension. A tired-sounding woman said, "Tossing and Flouncing, this is Nora." I think she detected a smirk in my voice, because before I could ask a complete question she transferred me to a guy in Drooling who kept calling me "Slick." I asked him if drooling is really such a national problem that it merits funds for research, and he started spouting bizarre statistics at me. I was skeptical. "Drownings?" I said. "In bed? Come on. Wouldn't you wake up before you—"

He abruptly put me on hold and I listened to a recording of the House Committee on Aging snoring in six-part harmony. They were pretty good, actually, considering one of them sounded like a goat sitting on a train whistle. Not that I could swear to exactly what that sounds like—it was just an impression.

The Drooling guy came back on the line and told me to hold on, he was going to transfer me to Oversleeping. It rang a dozen times and nobody answered, so I got sent back to a menu. I pressed the number for Morning Breath and spoke to a lady who had what sounded like a Lego rolling around in her mouth. I asked her about it. She said it was a mint, adding, "If you'd heard half the tragic stories I've heard, you'd understand."

"Don't tell me morning breath causes fatalities," I said.

"Dozens," she said. "Limburger, jalapeños, chittlins. People just don't know the dangers."

"This is getting a little far-fetched," I said. "To hear you people tell it, sleeping is as risky as hang-gliding. How dangerous can it be?"

"You want dangerous?" she said, "I'll transfer you to Hogging the Covers."

NEW YORK (NUR)—Federal anti-terrorism funding for Vermont rose from $31 per person to $32.45 last week when four people left the state, while New York's per capita funding fell from $5.47 to $5.38 when the population of Ghazi Khuzpur, Pakistan, immigrated to Schenectady.

New York's mayor continued to rail against what he called the "disgrace" of Congress allocating security funds to low-population areas instead of favoring densely populated, more probable terrorist targets like New York City. "I've never seen a terrorist with a map of a cornfield in his pocket," the mayor said.

An official from the Homeland Security Department (HSD) met with the mayor for four hours trying to get him to remember what kind of maps the terrorists he saw had been carrying. "It might not seem important at the time," the official said on condition of anonymity. "But any little detail might be a part of the puzzle." He said the mayor couldn't remember specifics, but that there were definitely no maps of crops, scrub brush, or anything else west of the Holland Tunnel.

The mayor pulled New York City from the National Association of Counties to protest the group's opposition to the measure that would funnel more security money to more populous states. To illustrate the mayor's point, an aide pointed out that Wyoming is getting $38 per person in anti-terrorism funds, almost twice the amount most residents spend on ammunition every weekend. In a telephone interview, the mayor of Gillette, Wyoming, said that the members of his church were considering pooling their HSD money to purchase a shoulder-fired Stinger missile.

Meanwhile the Department of Defense recently completed an exhaustive study that listed every known possible threat to the United States and ranked them by likelihood. The study ranked a terrorist strike in Wyoming just below an amphibious assault on Idaho by Uruguay, and slightly above a suicide bombing of the World's Largest Ball of Twine in Cawker City, Kansas.

The study also showed that the greatest threat facing Vermont (pop. 86) is not a terrorist attack, but rather desertion for lack of interest.

BAD BORDERLINE BEHAVIOR

My wife and I keep celebrating the many ways we've simplified our lives since we moved to Kentucky from L.A., and near the top of the list is the Louisville airport, which is like "Mayberry Airport and Sandwich Shop" compared to the Third-World morass of LAX. I've flown out of efficient little SDF a lot, thankfully, since you can't make a living as a comedian staying at home. It's easy to get people to come over for a few drinks and laughs, but it's tacky to ask them to pay.

I've worked on several cruise ships lately, and recently stepped off a plane in a small Caribbean nation whose economy is based entirely on selling mementos that horrify you the moment you unpack them at home. A skinny uniformed guard with a huge military hat looked at my passport and said, "Are you traveling on beezaness or pleajure?" Being punch-drunk and goofy after the red-eye from Chicago, I quipped, "Actually my business is traveling to give pleasure."

Since his job was to hear one of only two answers to the same question 1,357 times a day, I thought he might enjoy a break from the monotony. Wrong. Border guards love monotony, pray for spirit-sapping sameness, and thrive on soul-killing boredom, because anything out of the ordinary means paperwork, possibly even standing.

He glowered at me through thundercloud eyebrows, squinted at my passport, and said, "You think this is funny, Meester Drayderlin?"

He mangled my name so acrobatically while peering up from under the eaves of that two-story military lid that I just lost it. I tried to stifle the laugh, resulting in one of those whoopee-cushion, nostril-flapping nose blasts— *phlppplplsshhnnerkk!* and, realizing there could be inconvenient consequences, immediately tried to recover. "Hnuhh! Sorry, gnuh! I'm sorry," I babbled, struggling to keep a straight face. "No disrespect intended, sir, really, I'm very sorry!" I kept apologizing non-stop, afraid that if I gave him the slightest opening he'd utter some Ricky Ricardo beaut that would send me into a whooping hysteria, and my nose was still burning from the first top-kill operation.

He watched me blather, no doubt hoping I wouldn't say anything outright psychotic or he'd have to fill out a form. I wrapped up my kow-towing tirade with, "I'm a comedian headed to work on a cruise ship, so when I said my business is traveling to give pleasure, I meant I travel around making people laugh, so, heh, I was just—it was a joke. I'm very sorry."

There was a long, tense pause when I assumed he was reading my body language, trying to decide if I was a national threat, and whether to summon armed personnel. He said, "You have fruits or veggie tables, Meester Draydelin?" and I bit down on the side of my tongue so hard it made me tear up. I prayed blood wouldn't join the tears, inviting more questions. I fought down the murderous laugh-bubble expanding in my esophagus by focusing on the brim of his seven-liter chapeau and picturing a jail cell with the skeleton of an American smart-alec chained to the wall. I shook my head, not wanting to risk breathing, and he handed me my passport.

In the taxi to the hotel, I realized I had dodged what could have been a major international hassle and vowed to keep my sarcastic comments to myself when I had a ship to catch the very next day. I checked in, and the lady at reception asked me how many room keys I would need. "Twenty-seven," I said. "I met some musicians on the beach."

What could she do? I was already in the country.

CHICKEN BACKS TO BASICS

If you are a vegetarian or vegan, stop reading this now or we can't be held responsible if your rabbit-chow lunch makes a return appearance. Besides, it's just another wistful reflection on the days when steak and sunshine were good for you, bacon and eggs were the law, and a *passenger-side airbag* was your mother-in-law. Oh, we'll probably make a joke about not even knowing how to spell *cholesterol* back then—so really, you've heard it all before, go have a nice sprout-and-mozzarella on nine-grain bread.

Terrific. Okay. If you live in the South, chicke . . .

Ahem. You herbivores just move along, now, there's nothing more you can do here, you've made your points and we couldn't agree more: the beef bidness is murder, salt pork in the collards will slam your arteries shut with an audible slap, and we wish everybody would stop eating animals and love them like you do. Really. Why, we're going to decry things here that you've already decried your eyes out about, so don't make us preach to the choir about shoebox-bred veal and swine rights. We think humans are pretty darned uppity to go around eating their fellow warm-blooded earthlings, and the back of our van is just *covered* with bumper-stickers that make flesh-eaters nauseous and McDonalds grit its big ole yellow teeth. So we'll see you later, and give our love to Rainbow.

All righty. Here's the deal on eating chicken backs, a great Southern tradition:

Rule Number One: *Don't do it on a first date*, even if you happen to find the only restaurant outside Nairobi that serves them. Chicken backs are best eaten alone or among people who have seen you at your worst and still let you in the house.

The reason is simple: If you are eating a chicken back properly, regardless of how elegantly you're groomed and dressed, you will still look like you're hunkered over a twitching carcass, tensed to repel larger predators. Which is why The Colonel doesn't serve them and how McNuggets came to be—people like to think of "chicken" as a substance, like jello or peanut butter. They like to think of it as something you can pick off a tree, or maybe mine, like gypsum. They don't like to be reminded that their nine-piece extra-crispy dinner once had a brain stem and a boyfriend—maybe even plans for the future.

Now, when you tear into a chicken back (and that's the only way to eat one—using silverware is like using pliers to eat spaghetti), you're going to get messy, so just plan for it and you'll be okay. A good rule of thumb is one napkin for each hand, one for your mouth, and two for your shoes. Keeping a moistened beach towel handy is recommended when you can't shower right away.

Let's dig in: pick up the back by the handle provided. Now locate those delightful little oval nuggets nestled beside the spine, pop them out and suck them off your thumbs before they can bounce away and hit your shoes (Hmm. Did anyone else just hear someone faint into a spinach salad with pine nuts and a light vinaigrette?).

Now nibble away the little morsels hugging the handle, much like you would eat corn on the spine . . . er, cob. That done, promise yourself you're going to consume nothing but bran and filtered water for the next twelve days. Good. Now you can fully enjoy those fat floppy wings of flesh flapping off the far end ("*Spap!*"—the unmistakable sound of a pale forehead hitting fresh berries in yogurt).

Before we separate the mere omnivores from the hard-core, blood-lusty carnivores, a final warning to the sprout crowd: stop now or forever hurl your peas.

Fine. Gentlemen, start your enzymes. Turn the backbone over to expose the dark underpinnings of the chicken chassis. Probe the deepest depression with your thumbnail (until someone invents a specialty tool, it'll have to do), puncture the slick membrane, extrude that dangly little organ with the tentacles, and slurp it down for an exquisite burst of liver flavor ("*Splotch!*"—definitely the sound of prominent cheekbones hitting Eggplant Parmesan).

The vertebrae vanquished, the temptation is to lick your fingers and everything else you can reach without breaking local ordinances. Don't. Look up, and you'll notice that everyone in the room is already staring at you. Any more grooming with your tongue will start somebody easing toward the tranquilizer gun.

So use your napkin and fingerbowl, if available. Then clear your palate with a slice of ginger, a bite of rice, or a spoonful of sautéed squirrel brains . . . . Sorry. You have to watch these tofu types, or they'll read every word.

As long as we're on the subject of soul food heartily enjoyed by Southerners, I thought you'd get a kick out of this. Would you believe there's a Collard Green Festival in Ayden, N.C., every year, and they ask for submissions for a collection of poems about collards? I thought it would be fun to write one, and it was published in one of the collections.

Heavenly Greens

Adam and Eve called up to God,
And the Lord said, "What's all this
   squawkin'?"
Their fig leaves trembled and their elbows
   shook,
Eve whispered, "You do the talkin'!"

Adam said, "Lord, please don't get us wrong,
'Cause The Garden is just plum peachy.
We're tickled that you did such a heckuva
   job,
And we don't want to come off as preachy.

'Cause we don't believe in all Creation
'There's a planet as fine as this'un,
But we've talked it out amongst ourselves
And we feel like something is missin'.

There's some mighty fine eatin',

the squash and the corn,
The melons, the blackberry wine.
The home-grown tomaters and the sweet
    potaters,
And the grits, of course, are divine.

And, Lord, as much as we love the okra,
When it's slimy and easily swallered,
We can't help but wonder why You didn't
    create
Just a truck-patch or two of collards."

The sky split apart and lightning flashed,
And the thunder began to roll.
Then the Lord appeared in the midst of it all
Eating greens from a golden bowl.

He said, "I knew you'd get wind of it sooner
    or later,
When we cook it the smell is incredible;
And the taste of pot likker, sopped up with
    biscuits,
Makes everything else seem inedible.

But my children, there are some things
Mere mortals can't have,
'Cause a few things you just can't improve.
For collards are perfect, like Heaven, you see,
So it's one thing I just can't approve."

He took a huge bite, then started to leave,
When Eve stepped in front of old Adam.
"Wait a minute," she yelled, "you're probably
    right,
But there's one way you might not have
        had 'em!"

God shined upon Eve a benevolent smile,
And He said, "Well, at least you're not shy."
The heavenly greens He placed at her feet,
With a wink He said, "Give it a try."

Angels and seraphim all watched her work,
And one said, "How unorthodox!
She's thrown something in with collards,
    y'all!"
A plump cherub said, "It's ham hocks!"

It bubbled and simmered, a sweet mist
    arose,
And finally Eve said, "They're done."
God sent an angel to fetch him a bowl,
Then they all flew away toward the sun.

Next day Adam yelled, "Honey, come here
    quick!"
And, of course, she faithfully follered.
And there in the valley, all bushy and
    green,
Was a crop of beautiful collards.

God's voice boomed, "Children, it took six
    days
To make Heaven and Earth and the seas,
And it was all good, the meadows and
    woods,
The pears, the berries, the peas.

The fishes and critters, they were good, too,
Impossible to imitate.
So you see, I've made some good things in
    My day,
But, honey, them collards were great!"

NEW YORK (NUR)—After Continental Airlines fired a female ticket agent for refusing to wear make-up, male flight attendants are suing the company, saying they should at least be allowed to wear, quote, "the tiniest bit of eyeliner and a little blush." Head flight attendant Lance DuBois said it's outrageous that female flight attendants are *required* to wear make-up, while he is prohibited from wearing it, "no matter how pasty and washed-out I look." Lamented DuBois, "Just a hint of base could do wonders. This little moustache covers only so much."

A Continental spokesman said the company allowed male attendants to wear make-up in an experimental program last year, but abandoned the program when too many of them arrived at work resembling Charro and Liza Minelli.

SANTA MONICA (NUR)—A California woman is in satisfactory condition tonight after surgeons removed her thong bikini from her Fallopian tubes. A hospital spokesman said the 23-year-old flight attendant was sunbathing in the tiny swimsuit when a fighter jet broke the soundbarrier overhead, causing her to tense up and absorb the garment.

HOLLYWOOD (NUR)—Universal Pictures says its next film will be an urban thriller starring many new and established rap stars. The as-yet-untitled film will showcase Ice Cube and Ice T, along with newcomers Ice Tray, Ice Bag, Ice Machine, and the female lead, Ice Chest.

DAMASCUS (NUR)—Military leaders in Syria denied today that they have used chemical weapons against the rebellious Shiite Muslims and invited the enemy to inspect certain facilities in the battle zone. They invited 200,000 Shiites to stand, quote, "In a bunch" near the border on Wednesday and "Wait around for awhile."

PORTLAND, OR (NUR)—A black woman in Portland, Oregon, has admitted she staged up to 20 so-called hate crimes against herself, including burning crosses on her own lawn, to get attention. At her arraignment, Althea Cooley shouted racial epithets at herself and was removed from the courtroom when a shoving match broke out among her.

NEW YORK (NUR)—David Letterman scored a huge victory in the late-night talk-show wars this week, announcing that Janet Jackson's breasts will be his guests on Thursday. A spokesman said that although Janet is on concert tour, her breasts happened to be in town doing a photo shoot for the cover of *Freshwater Fisherman*, the only national magazine on which her breasts have not yet appeared. Last week Jackson's doctor said the singer's breasts were suffering from exhaustion and overexposure.

CINCINATTI (NUR)—The makers of the Ken and Barbie dolls are under fire again. Critics recently accused Mattel Toys of unfairly stereotyping women by having the talking Barbie say, "Math class is tough." Now the object of protest is the new talking Ken doll, which says, "Wash the dishes later, bitch, I said come to bed now." A company spokesman some fanatics will find sexism in anything.

STANDUP

Some of my standup bits don't translate well to the printed page because I'm so physical and use my rubber face so much on stage (and singing doesn't translate at all). On the other end of the scale, Henny Youngman's deadpan delivery of "Take my wife—please," doesn't depend much on physicality for the laugh. I know you didn't pick up this book hoping for an essay on standup, but hopefully you'll be one of the many people who are fascinated by the "backstage" lore of the craft. Anyway, after many years of practicing and watching standup, I've come to the conclusion that comics usually fall into one of three basic categories:

1. The person whose stage persona is pretty much the same as their actual personality—Bill Maher, Ellen DeGeneres, Jerry Seinfeld, Jay Leno. You don't see them doing other voices or accents or morphing into other characters (can you even imagine Jerry suddenly doing an excited Mexican trying to sell him a souvenir? Nooo), and they use funny gestures and mime very sparingly if at all. In other words, they don't really act much because they're more comfortable just talking in their own voices.

2. The comic who becomes another character totally unlike their actual personality when he/she goes on stage—Gilbert Gottfried's screamer, e.g., "Bobcat" Goldthwait and his whacked-out druggie character. Robin Williams is fairly laid-back and shy before he becomes that wildly frenetic character on stage. I know a hilarious, childless, gay comedienne who always performs as an often-divorced, harried mother of several snot-nosed kids—a 100% made-up fictional character that's nothing like her.

3. Comics like me—and there are legions, from the late George Carlin to Eddie Murphy to virtuosos like Lily Tomlin and Whoopi—who transform into dozens of characters during a performance. I routinely step out of my own persona and pretend to be a distraught Arab militant, a redneck truck driver, a female store clerk, my wife, and even a broken record player.

Since my comedy is so physical, I've had a lot of success with YouTube videos and invite you to type my name in the Search box on the site and lots of funny stuff will come up. My "Ode to Forgetfulness" has gotten more than 3 million views at last check, and "What Women Need" had edged past 30,000 last I looked. You might also look up "World Goose Chase," "Buford's House of Liver," "Plastic Wrap Blues," and "I Don't Respect You Now."

But if you wanted to go online you wouldn't be sitting here with a book, would you? So if you'll imagine me saying the following on stage, I'll try to tickle your ribs using nothing but ink on paper.

BLESS YOUR HEART

I love to get down to Mississippi because it's one of the only places left where you can get your heart properly blessed. (*Heavy Southern accent*) "They didn't bring that coffee to you yet, honey? Well bless your heart. You had to drag that stuff over here all by yourself? *Bless your heart.*" I used to live in L.A., and let me tell you, it's a *No Blessing Zone.* Bless a heart, go to jail out there. Not in Mississippi: There it's a wonderful sentiment, and the great thing about it is you can say *anything about anybody* as long as you *tag* it with that: "Pore thang, he aint got the sense God give a mud turtle, bless his heart. Ugly as a bald-headed bullfrog, bless his heart. I hope they get that child some braces, she could eat watermelon through a picket fence, bless her heart.

POSSUMS AND CROWS

I had all my neighbors in L.A. blessing each other's hearts before I left, and it was nice. They all knew where I grew up, of course, so whenever there was a *critter* crisis of any kind, "Oh, don't call Animal Control, call Mack, he grew up down South, running barefooted through the swamps, eating squirrels right out of the trees." Which is ridiculous, of course. We shot 'em first. One day my neighbor Helen called and said, "Mack! There's a possum caught on my back porch and he can't find his way out!" I said, "Okay, Helen, what do you need from me? A *recipe*?" That's the first thing I thought of, you know, is he scrawny or does he have some meat on him? She said, "What can I *do*?" and of course I'm thinking *slow roast with sweet potatoes*—hey, I watch *Top Chef!* But people in L.A. don't want to hear about eating little woodland creatures. That's the land of Disney out there, so they think when we're not looking, wild animals wear aprons and speak English.

Another time my neighbor Irv called and said, "Mack, there's a crow with a broken wing in my backyard, can you help me out," and I said, "Sure, this is an easy one." So I got my Crow first-aid kit . . . a ball bat and a Hefty bag, and I headed on over and he said, "*No*, no, I don't want to do that, I want to take him to the vet." The *vet*?! I said, "Irv, you don't spend money to fix *broke crows*!" He insisted, so I said, "Okay, here's what we'll do. I'll put him in this box and take him back to my place, and I'll do the best I can, and if it makes it through the night, then tomorrow we'll take it to the vet." (*long pause, slow grin*) He didn't make it through the night. Bless his heart. Poor thing was despondent and when I wasn't looking he committed suicide with a pellet gun. I felt terrible.

WHAT WOMEN NEED

I really hit a nerve with audiences when I started performing this bit, and it's been a joy to work it and polish it and watch men nudging their giggling wives in the audience when I perform it. Couples just get a huge kick out of it as they recognize just how much STUFF she needs to get through the day.

I had a practice wife—*brrrr*! But now that I've found my Final Wife, I'm determined to keep her, and we've been married since 1996, (*do the math*). People ask me what's the secret to a long relationship, and I figured it out: you have to know what your mate *needs* and help provide it, and men's and women's needs are so *different* that it's not easy to do. Men need a *lot more* of some things, women need a *lot more* of other things.

And over the years, my wife has taught me that she needs, for example, more calcium . . . iron, time in the bathroom, heart-to-heart communication, hand holding, hand wringing, hand lotion, ointments, unguents, emollients, cotton balls, phone time with her mother, her sisters, her friends, her hairdresser. Lipstick, lip gloss, lip balm, lip liner, shoes for every *conceivable* situation, products to take care of her hair, eyes, skin, fingernails, toenails, cracked heels, exfoliation and feminine needs, unwanted hair and odors, constant assurance that her butt is *exactly* the right size, little porcelain and glass things, candles, mirrors, picture frames, things made out of gold, silk, and *wicker*, pillows of *every conceivable* shape and size, detailed information about the neighbors' personal lives, time to express her feelings, time to discuss why you have *no* feelings or the *wrong* feelings, time to correct *all* of your imperfections and rehabilitate you, an elegant little purse that holds lipstick and a credit card, and an epic purse that holds Walgreen's.

(*Here I pause, take sip of water, then:*)

Matching accessories, baskets, loofahs, potpourri, hundreds of tiny bottles with mysterious stuff in them, dozens of pretty little boxes with *nothing* in them, and an occasional girl's night out with a gay guy who can dance . . . and that's about it, guys. If you can remember that, you're good.

Of course, men have their own needs. For example, men need a lot more televised sports . . . (*pause*). And that's about it, really.

TALKING TO THE DOG

How many of you have a dog you love? They're great, aren't they? Unlike the people in your life, they're always happy to see you, aren't they? That's why we love 'em so much. They don't hold grudges. I heard about a guy who accidentally locked his wife and his dog in one of those self storage units. A few hours later when he realized what he'd done, he rushed back and let them out and guess what? Only one of them was happy to see him. His dog wagged his tail and licked his hand, and his wife . . . didn't.

My wife and I both talk to our dog, but in totally different ways. I'll say, "Kiko, stay," or "Hey, sweet girl," or "Get that squirrel!" And that's about it. Not my wife. She carries on *lengthy,* one-way conversations and *interrogates* her:

(*Here I mimic my wife looking down at the dog*) "Kiko? Are you hungry? Why didn't you eat what's in your bowl? Don't stare at me like that. I'm not going to give you anymore until you eat what's in your bowl. Why won't you eat it?"

(*I look up at the audience again*) Kiko takes the Fifth—every time. We've had her for eleven years, and as far as I know she's never made a single comment, but my wife apparently thinks that one day she's going to spontaneously start speaking English:

(*Looking down again*) "Aren't you hungry? Are you holding out for chicken parts? I gave you chicken parts this morning. You're not getting any more until you finish this, okay? I'm not throwing away any more food, do you understand?"

Of course, she never tells me when she's

going to be talking to the dog, so half the time I think she's talking to me, and it can get confusing:

"Come in here!" (*I jog in*)

"Don't do that!" (*I look both ways*)

"Do you want a treat?" (*I grin stupidly and nod my head*)

"Get down!" (*I squat down, frightened*)

It occasionally causes a little dust-up, you know. (*Agitated*) "Why can't I have any chicken parts? I bought the dern chicken parts, I'll eat chicken parts if I want to. In fact I'm going to make myself a big, fat chicken parts sandwich right now!"

ON SALE

I'm the breadwinner of the house, and my wife's a wonderful homemaker, artist, and wife, but I'm just amazed at how much money she brings into the house. For example, last weekend she bought $480 worth of stuff . . . on SALE! The money is just *pouring* into the house! At 40% off, I don't know where we're going to put all the cash! I have to sweep it out of the hall so we can walk to the bedroom. Sometimes toward the end of the month, I'll look at the books and say, "Honey, it's going to be tight this month, I don't know if we're going to be able to make all these payments, *thank God there's a sale at Macy's!* You go get it, baby!"

FLYING

It's no fun to fly anymore, with all the security, and the five-dollar cookies and seven-dollar beers. I was going through security the other day, the guy asks me if I have any photographic film or sharp objects in my carry-on bag. I said, "No-o-o, but I do have a photograph of an ice pick. Is that a problem?" You know what scares me? He didn't know. Had to go check with his supervisor.

So I got to the gate, and the agent took my ticket and said, "Have a *great flight.*" A great flight? Come on. I'm sorry, but there's no such thing as a great flight. There's *miserable*, and a *tolerable* flight, depending on how close to the baby you're sitting. But there're really no great flights, are there? Did you ever pick somebody up at the airport and say, "How was your flight?" and they say, "Oh, man, it was a *great flight.* They handed out pizza and tequila shooters, *(dancing)* there was a conga line in the aisle, a Kardashian gave me a lap dance! It was a *great flight.*"

I don't require my flight be *great.* It just has to be . . . *complete.* I won't be doing business with *We Almost Made It* Airlines.

Don't get me wrong, I'm not scared of flying—I've got enough miles to go to another planet. The only thing that scares me a little is those tiny little claustrophobic restrooms with those seven megaton sucking toilets. *SLRRP!* I've lost like three pairs of contacts in those things. I'm scared it's going to suck me in and spit me out over Oklahoma, so some farmer would be talking about me on the evening news: (*hick accent*) "Wail, it was a big chunk of blue ice, it was trailin' toilet paper, and it was screamin' when it hit the barn." I don't want to go out like that.

Anybody ever been on a cruise ship? They have the same kind of toilet, but they'll have a sign behind it that says, "Do not flush while seated." HA! Boy, you don't have to tell ME twice. I was on one ship where a poor guy flushed while seated. He beat us to Aruba by two hours.

ALAMO

I was just in San Antonio, great city, very pretty, and historic, too, of course. Got to see the Alamo, quite an interesting place. And since I was just there I remember the history: Back in 1836, thousands of Mexicans overran a badly outnumbered group of American defenders, and in the 175 years since then, I can't see that the border patrol has improved that much, frankly. Yeah, they're doing re-enactments of that every ten, fifteen minutes, if you know where to go.

CANNIBALS

Talk about weird cultures. I saw a *National Geographic* special about the islands in the South Pacific, and it was fascinating. On islands like Fiji and Tonga, there was still cannibalism going on as late as the 1920's. Unbelievable. So when we were going through Prohibition, and they were trying to keep us from having a drink with our friends and neighbors, in Fiji they were trying to get them to stop *eating* their friends and neighbors! And one phrase in the article really stood out for me: They said it was a "normal part of life." Well, sure, unless *you* were the Businessman's Special! You'd have to be pretty careful if you were invited to a cookout. You'd hate to get there and find out they took you along because it's *pot luck*, brr. "Yeah, sorry, Nogulu, you were available, we needed a side dish . . . but don't worry, it's *perfectly normal*."

Right. And can you imagine what dining out was like?

(*I do a lilting, rather effeminate voice*) Let me tell you about our specials today. Larry was a champion swimmer, excelled in water sports, so he's our *Surf and Turf* today. Fresh off a lifeboat we have Celeste, she was an exotic dancer in Poughkeepsie, so if you're in the mood for a *New York strip* . . . . And finally, Eugene was a big boy, very slow runner, so he's our *Catch of the Day*.

GAS PUMP LABELS

I was filling up at a gas station the other day, and it's kind of boring, you flip the latch on the nozzle, nothing to do, this is how bored I was: I actually read the labels on the gas pump, and I'm glad I did because it was entertaining. The first one said, "In case of fire, do not remove nozzle from vehicle." Probably good advice, but, I have to be honest, in case of *FIRE* at a *GAS* station? I'm going to be a little busy removing my *ASS* from the *PREMISES*. (*flamethrower sound effect, swoosh!*) "Oh, Lord, my car is engulfed in a fireball, I'm not trained in these matters, I certainly hope there are *some printed instructions* I can study!" No, if there's a fire and you're standing right on top of 10,000 gallons of gas in an underground tank, well, if you always wanted to go to the Bahamas, you just might get your wish. You talk about getting to Aruba in a *hurry!*

There was a label right under that one that said, "Gasoline can be harmful or fatal if swallowed," and I wondered, are we really saving the lives of hundreds of *brain dead morons* every year? I mean, seriously, if you pull up to a gas pump because you're thirsty, well, you shouldn't be driving. I know you shouldn't be reproducing, for sure. I don't know if putting that sign up there is really a good thing for society. I don't mean we should put something misleading like, "Gasoline provides nine essential vitamins" or anything like that, but just leave it off. Because if you're dumb enough to suck gasoline out of a nozzle, you're doing us a favor by tidying up the gene pool, you know, thinning the herd, reducing our carbon footprint, one moron at a time.

HONEYMOON

My wife and I met a couple at a party the other night and we asked them how they met, and they kind of laughed and gave each other funny looks. Turns out they met when the guy, would you believe, was on his *honeymoon* with his first wife! Man! Talk about awkward. When do you think he had the first inkling that his marriage might be in trouble? Not a lot of guys think of their honeymoon as an opportunity to *meet women!* You have to admire the woman, too. She had some nerve, didn't she? She's like, "Oh, on your honeymoon, huh? So . . . will you spend the *whole time* with her, or are you seeing other people?" Then when they got married and went on *their* honeymoon, she probably just handcuffed him to the bed, whattya think? "Yeah, you'll be stickin' pretty close to me, *hound dog*, don't be getting any ideas."

SEX CHANGE PREACHER

I read about this preacher over in Iowa who decided he was a woman trapped in a man's body. So he took the hormones, had the operation, which is a pretty drastic thing, I mean, *whack.* Ouch. Then, about six months later, uh oh, he decided that he wasn't a woman trapped in a man's body after all, now he wants to *go back to being a man!* Hmm. Well, folks, this is obviously a case of a *moron* being trapped in the body of an *idiot!* I hope he kept the *trimmings* from that first operation. Because how many organ donors do you think are going to be lining up for *this* one? You thought it was tough finding a KIDNEY, brother, *whoo!* Guys who fill out that organ donor card are going, "Eyes? Sure. Liver? No problem. Um, no, Mr. Winkie stays with me, I keep the Big Unit, okay?"

Not me, I'd give mine up in a second. I like the idea that after I'm gone, I'll still be getting some action. Think about it, if you agreed to give up all your organs except your bidness, when you got to the next world, you might just be, well, a *dick.*

ONE RIFE TO RIV

I've been hired to help write a number of live shows and TV shows and even movies. I looked back over a lot of material I've written for various projects, and this one really resonated with me. Barry Manilow's personal manager hired me to write some sketches for a variety show he was trying to get on the air (it didn't pan out), and this was one of them. Jamie and I actually performed it on stage a few times in a two-man show we did once, and we got a great, warm response every time. Hope you enjoy it.

BOB AND FRED—MIDDLE-AGED BLUE-COLLAR TYPES—DRINK BEER IN A BAR. THE WAY THEY'RE DRESSED, AND A FEW DETAILS AROUND THE BAR INDICATE THAT WE'VE BEEN TRANSPORTED A HUNDRED YEARS OR MORE INTO THE FUTURE.

FRED: Kids! Jeez. Can you figure 'em? Ricky comes to me yesterday, wants me to double his allowance. I said hell no, a thousand a week is plenty for a ten-year-old.

BOB: Yeah. It's amazin'. Five years ago a kid could take in a movie and get a burger for, what, a couple hundred bucks? Now you gotta take out a federal loan to get popcorn.

FRED: Yeah. And kids ain't satisfied just to climb a tree for a good time anymore. Christ, ya gotta give 'em the moon.

BOB: Yeah. That's what Michael wants for graduation.

FRED: What's that?

BOB: The moon. Senior trip. (WHINING) "Everybody's going but me, Dad."

FRED: Yeah, I know what you mean.

BOB: I mean Ginny turned 16 this week and already she wants her own place. She's got her own 85-inch Optiscreen, a brand new transascope we gave her for Christmas, she's the only 16-year-old around with a Sex-a-Toodle, and she wants to move out.

FRED: Whoa. Ginny's got a Sex-a-Toodle?

BOB: Hey, Fred, wake up! It's not 2040 anymore, get with it. Kids grow up quicker these days. She'd just sneak around and use somebody else's.

FRED: I hear those things really do the trick. Harriet's been after me to get her one, but jeez, we can hardly afford wood for the car anymore.

BOB: Aw, you can pick up a good used one for half a million. Check out your yard sales.

FRED: I know, but what about me! Heck, if I want to get it on more than once a month Harriet calls me an animal. It's like trying to get into Fort friggin' Knox, f' cryin' out loud. If she stays plugged into a Sex-a-Toodle all day long, she won't need me for nothin' but openin' pickle jars.

BOB: Nah, Fred, there's ways around that. I got one for Gloria, and I put these cheap xantonium cells in it that blow out every few days. Soon as it shuts down she goes into withdrawal, tries to get into *my* pickle jar, you know what I'm sayin'?

FRED: Yeah? Yeah. I could—Nah, Harriet majored in electro-nuclear physics. She'd figure that one out like *that*!

BOB: Yeah, you're probably right. Hey. So get yourself one, too.

FRED: They make 'em for men?

BOB: Do they make—? Where you been, Fred?! The Supreme Court just ruled you could marry one.

FRED: I thought that was blow-dryers.

BOB: Nah. Remember when IBM and Frederick's of Hollywood merged?

FRED: Yeah?

BOB: They came out with a whole line of

computerized sex-a-ma-thingies. You know, Digital Darlene, Vacuum-Tube Vinnie. Specialty units like Tommy Two-Tongues. Anything you want, Fred, plug it in and va-va-vooWAABBBA! You'd be doing your wife a favor.

FRED: I don't know, Bob. Seems like me and Harriet hardly talk to each other anymore as it is. We used to talk about her job, but this laser transmogrification stuff is way over my head. Heck, we used to cook breakfast together every morning. Now she just programs the proton accelerator. Damn thing can make omelets I never even heard of. I come home from work and there's always something better than me on TV. I mean, I don't know about you, Bob, but I can't compete with 800 channels and Hi-Def 3-D Sensa-Feel reception. Anything you can imagine! I mean, the Mardi Gras channel from Rio! Nude volleyball from Sweden, for God's sake! Now she's watching a goddamn Japanese soap opera every day! Japanese!

BOB: Which one is that, *One Rife to Riv*? Heh heh.

FRED: It ain't funny, Bob!

BOB: Okay, okay, sorry, jeez!

FRED: (STEAMED) We used to putter around in the yard together, ya know? Pullin' weeds, mowin' the grass, I used to love that smell. Now with all this—this miracle spray crap, I don't lift a finger and my lawn looks like a putting green! You gotta go to a goddamn museum to see a weed anymore! (GRABBING BOB) Do you know what a great feelin' it was gettin' your hands dirty, pulling crabgrass out by the throat?! You was DOIN' somethin'!

BOB: Fred! Fred! Hey! Cool down, buddy, it's okay! It's okay.

FRED: I'm sorry. I'm okay. it just . . . gets to me sometimes. I think I was born fifty years too late, Bob.

BOB: Fifty years, huh? Believe me, my friend, you wouldn't want to go back if you could really remember how it was. I mean the advances we've made—

FRED: Advances?! Advan—? Before I talk to my kids I gotta pry 'em loose from some video-laser-space-craft-battle simulator machine.

BOB: Those things are educational, Fred, and besides, it keeps 'em off the streets.

FRED: I talk to my wife twice a week during commercial breaks.

BOB: A blessing, Fred, believe me, enjoy it.

FRED: I can't even take a drive anymore without my car bitching at me about seat belts or helium pressure or (ROBOT VOICE) "Exceeding the recommended altitude for this sector."

BOB: Oh, sure. I suppose you miss the good old days, when you had to think of everything yourself? Remember tires? Big rubber things pumped fulla air? Ha ha! And gas? Remember when you used to run out of gas ten miles from nowhere?

FRED: (SMILING DREAMILY) Yeah. God, what a night that was. Me and Harriet got engaged that night.

BOB: Yeah? Engaged in what, Fred? Heh heh.

FRED: (UNFAZED) I took her to see a little waterfall on a creek. We walked half an hour through the woods and when we got back somebody had siphoned my tank dry. We wrapped up in a sleeping bag and talked all night. (PAUSE) You ever watch the sun come up when you got absolutely nothing else to do but enjoy it, Bob? There ain't nothing like it. Nothing like it.

BOB: (DREAMY) Yeah. I know what you mean. You can watch a different sunrise every day on channel 723. Last week I was watchin' one and—

FRED: (SMILING) Bob?

BOB: Yeah, Fred?

FRED: (RISING) I'll see you—well, I'll see you when I see you.

BOB: Where you going?

FRED: Someplace very special, Bob. Nowhere. Me and Harriet are gonna take . . . a walk.

BOB: (STUNNED) A wa—A walk?! (POINTS TO WALL TV) But Fred, it's—it's prime time.

FRED: (NODDING, SMILING) Boy. You never said a truer word, my friend. It sure is.

AS FRED STROLLS OUT, SMILING, BOB SITS THERE PUZZLED, AND WE SLOWLY

FADE TO BLACK

Buster Babcock's

BACHELOR

BRIEFS

A Suvival Guide
for Single Guys

* * *

If You Think "Domestic Bliss" is Any Beer Made in America, Then This Guide Is For You

I wrote and voiced "Bachelor Briefs with Buster Babcock" for Premiere for a couple of years, and he was a really popular, hilariously over-the-top character. We've all been acquainted with a few "Busters" and know they can be as charming and amusing as they are exasperating. They're the kind of guys who think their livers and lungs are indestructible and that moderation is for sissies. If they're not partying, they're recovering from one, and they shudder at the thought of committing more than a couple of therapeutic hours to any female for any reason. They know every housekeeping shortcut imaginable to keep their domiciles just neat and clean enough that a person of the female persuasion won't take one look and a whiff and run out screaming.

For all his rough edges, Buster is a lovable character because he's committed to his lifestyle and genuinely wants to help his fellow bachelors enjoy the sporting life. So if you're a guy, you might actually pick up some helpful tips. And if you're a woman, well, who knows? Maybe you'll get a little valuable insight into what makes the grosser sex tick.

Housekeeping
☆ ☆ ☆ ☆

Dust Bunnies: A Natural Resource

Don't clean out dust bunnies—harvest them. They make great packing material, good insulation, even decent little throw pillows if you stuff them into freezer bags.

Getting By
★ ★ ★ ★

Getting More Weeks out of Your Socks

Cut the stinky parts out of your socks and just leave a thin strap to hold them on. You can wear them a hundred times between washings.

Hound-Dogging
☆ ☆ ☆ ☆

Life-Saving Bed Linens

Bed linens with bold prints camouflage all kinds of trace evidence, from the deadly Short Hair to lipstick smears.

FUNNY SLIPPERS

Reminding you today that everything we love to do depends on some rain, so quit cussing the weather and remember that if God had intended for us to fish seven days a week, he wouldn't have invented women. Now, you might have noticed that women have this really weird, picky thing about keeping their floors clean, even though all we do is walk on 'em. So if you're going over to visit a new woman acquaintance, do what I do when it's been raining and everything's mushy outside: before you ring the doorbell, take your muddy shoes off and set them by the door. Then put on a pair of the stupidest slippers you can find—you know, the ones that look like rabbits or ducks or fuzzy bear paws or something. You'll get huge points for being neat, big laughs that'll put her in a real playful mood, and before you know it she'll wanta get into her slippers and jammies, too.

REMOTE CONTROL

Sometimes you just can't get out of watching TV with a woman, but I've figured out a pretty good way to maintain control of the remote, which is absolutely necessary if you're going to spend three hours on a couch fully clothed. Here's one technique that works for me: Pick up the remote and SLAP the table it was sittin' on and pretend to pick something up and go to the sink and wash your hands. Tell her you killed a spider, and she'll go "ewwww!" and then tell her spiders like to hide under the remote cause the battery keeps 'em warm. I didn't say it was true, I said it was effective, and women will believe anything about spiders OR batteries if it means they don't have to touch one.

Housekeeping
★ ★ ★ ★
Jock Motif

Had enough bitching about the socks and underwear on your bedroom floor? Buy a bunch and glue them down for a Jock Motif. Nobody will know where your design stops and your laziness begins.

Hound-Dogging
★ ★ ★ ★

Hand-y Reminder

If you go home from a party with somebody new, write her name on your hand before you go to bed to avoid an ugly scene in the morning. An ounce of prevention is better than a sure pounding.

Getting By
★ ★ ★ ★

Flexible Decorating Motif

Glue your girly pictures to the backs of some windmill and sailboat pictures, hang a string from the top, and the next surprise visit from your Mom won't be nearly so frantic.

Hound-Dogging
★ ★ ★ ★
Double Dinner Points

Ask the skinniest woman you're seeing out to dinner, and fill up on a couple of cheesburgers before you take her to one of those places that serve gigantic portions. Take your ten-point doggie bag home, and the next night serve a "home-cooked" candlight dinner to another woman.

Sexy Underwear

A real bachelor knows the only reason to go into Victoria's Secret is to hit on the sales clerks. That's right: *Never* buy sexy underwear for a woman unless you intend to marry her, which, for me anyway, means never buy sexy underwear for a woman. It just opens up a whole can of Pandora's worm boxes. See, us guys think of skimpy underwear as *sexy*— *ROWRR!*—but women think of sexy underwear as *intimate—BRRR!*, and that you want to get to know her better, when in fact, you just want to make it a little easier to remember that spread in *Playboy* so you can get up for the game, so to speak. It's not a real practical garment, anyway, since you get it off her as quick as possible, so she might have it for six months and only wear it a total of a coupla minutes. And any article of clothing you take off with your teeth just wears out quicker. So save yourself the trouble and money and tell her that her old gym shirt with the holes in it just drives you wild with desire.

Simple Pleasure

Today I wanta talk about an emotional and crucial aspect of every bachelor's life that's getting more complicated every day, and often leaves us confused and needing guidance to attain complete fulfillment. I am talking, of course, about beer, which used to be cold, foamy, full of big laughs and boogie woogie and tearful promises at 2 a.m. Now you've got 9,000 choices between ale or lager or some god-awful-sounding thing like pizner or Heifer-Whizzin', for God's sake. There used to be two flavors: regular and light. Now you've got honey-raspberry-wheat and pale double-wicked gooseberry cream porter and lord knows what-all, when all you want is a cold beer that'll wash down the dust, make your singing sound great and the women all look attractive in their own way. So here's my advice today: Simplify your life—learn to like it all, so when the only thing available is Old Fish Head Summer Beriberi Ale, you can pop one and join the fun, cause life's just too dern short to let hard choices come between you and man's second greatest pleasure.

The Single Guy Fraternity

You're a member in good standing if you think . . .

. . . "married life" is an oxymoron. You're either married, or you got a life.

. . . domestic bliss is any beer that's made in America.

. . . a wedding band is something you dance to.

. . . "lifetime commitment" means without the possibility of parole

. . . your "significant other" is the one you call when the other one's a significant distance out of town.

. . . "settling down" means in front of the TV with chips and beer.

Housekeeping
★ ★ ★ ★
Shower Terrarium

When the green stuff growing around your bathtub starts growing leaves, buy some plants to give it tropical ambience. Collect all resident amphibians before letting a female guest use the facilities.

Housekeeping

★ ★ ★ ★

Ironing Man Competition

Ironing is like sex: Never do it alone unless you absolutely have to. You'll only iron for a few seconds before she pushes you out of the way to do it *right*. Ask her if she thinks her girlfriend is going to marry that dentist, then watch sports highlights while she babbles and irons.

Hound-Dogging

★ ★ ★ ★

Her Pet: Do's and Don't's

DO make her think you love the little fur-ball.

DON'T let her catch you expressing your true feelings.

COACHING WOMEN

All right, I've got an important warning for you today if you're a good softball player: sooner or later, a woman is going to ask you to coach her team, which is just like an invitation to dive naked into a snake pit, so don't ever, ever, EVER agree to do it. So many things can go wrong I hardly know where to start. For example, if your tasty little shortstop finds out you've also been doing extra-curricular physical therapy with your left fielder, YOU will become the cut-off man, because you will be cut off for the rest of the season, take my word for it, and she will have no trouble HITTING the cut-off man, believe me. Also, God help you if you automatically pat your no-neck third baseman on the butt for a good play, 'cause her girlfriend with the Harley t-shirt and sideburns will tear out of the bleachers and have to be restrained by the whole dern infield while you're hidin' in the dugout from a WOMAN, for cryin' out loud, need I say more?

MORE SOFTBALL COACHING

You loyal listeners will remember that on my last segment I advised you guys not to coach a woman's softball team cause it's a regular minefield of horrors waiting to happen. If you weren't convinced before, here are a couple more reasons not to get dragged into it: if you're dating somebody who's not on the team, which is likely, she'll accuse you of nailing the whole infield on the sly, and will read an entire romance novel into everything you do at the ball field: You can't slap anybody on the butt for a good play, or call anybody Darlin', or even hug anybody after a big win without setting in motion a campaign of terror and sexual austerity. So, my advice is, if you've already been roped into coaching a girl's team, go ahead and try to nail the entire infield, cause you're gonna get accused of it anyway.

Housekeeping
★ ★ ★ ★

Leaf-Blower Magic

After the next major blowout at your place,
use a king-hell leaf blower to blast the place clean.
This also clears out stragglers.

Getting By
★ ★ ★ ★

Pine-Tree Deodorizers

Mix those pine-tree car deodorizers into the
dirty-clothes basket to keep sweaty socks and jocks
from stinking up the whole house. Just be sure
to pick them out if you grab some used stuff for a
quick game.

Hound-Dogging
★ ★ ★ ★
True Commitment: The Team

    Women do not understand the importance of softball. When the whining gets too bad, look deep into her eyes and say, "When I commit to something, I *stay* committed." It's a dirty trick, but hey, the guys are depending on you.

INCREDIBLE BASKET-SCRATCHING
BREAKTHROUGH

Boy, I'm excited about this one, guys, a helpful hint that will *change your life*. One of the truly masculine pleasures that guys can claim as their very own is scratching and rearranging, but pro baseball players are the only ones who can get away with it in public, because there's not any women on the field to chew them out about it, and as long as they keep bringing home the big bucks, their wives don't care what body parts they play with as long as they ain't on somebody else. Anyway, scratching in public was a real challenge until one day I accidentally busted out the right front pocket in my jeans. After about a week, I realized that I can just always carry my keys and pocketknife in my left front pocket. So now, as soon as I buy a pair of pants, I just cut that right pocket completely out for unobstructed access and discreet satisfaction. There you go! I mean, is that genius or what?!

Planning Your Easter Flu

Okay guys, Easter's closing fast, so I want to remind you that you'll probably get roped into hiding Easter eggs for your nieces and nephews, so now is a good time to start getting a stomach flu. Call a family member on Thursday night and tell 'em you've been feeling lousy and throwing up, and they'll chew your ear off about how awful it was when they got it. Ooo and ahh a lot and say, "Really?" a couple of times and ask them for advice and they'll give it 'til you want to smack 'em. Then on Friday, every time the phone rings, answer it like you're dying—you know, *ack-kk-hellooo*—and when it's a relative checking up on you, tell 'em your diarrhea got so bad you went to the doctor and he said it's a highly contagious flu-bug and you have to stay away from everybody for three days. Then leave a croaky message on your answering machine saying you're in bed, and that'll free up your Sunday to hang with the guys or look for an Easter honey-bunny. Okay, I'm outa time, and I hope you feel better by Memorial Day.

Hound-Dogging
★ ★ ★ ★
Pandora's Trash Can

Remember to empty your bathroom trashcan.
It contains more incriminating evidence of a female
nature than any other square foot in the house.

Hound-Dogging
★ ★ ★ ★
Valentine's Day Safety

Count up the women you have to please on
Valentine's Day and get them all the exact same
flowers and candy so you have one less set of facts
to keep straight.

Hound-Dogging
☆ ☆ ☆

The Designated Sister

You have to have a sister if you're going to fool around, because you can claim the hairpins and other physical evidence is hers. If you don't have a sister, bribe, blackmail, or beg someone to be your Designated Sister.

Sunscreen Do's and Don'ts

Man, I can't believe it, but summer's finally comin' on, so it's time for a few rules about puttin' on suntan lotion. First, let me answer the most frequently-asked question: Guys, it's okay to put lotion on each other if you're out in public, but there are some pretty dern rigid rules. Obviously, you can only put it on another guy's back, and don't stray too far below the shoulder blades or it'll start lookin' funny. If you rub lotion on a guy's face, chest or anywhere on his legs, go ahead and break it to your parents—you're gay. If you're slathering up a woman, the rules are determined by how well you know her and how well she *wants* you to know her. If your hand casually slips into no man's land, you'll know where you stand in pretty short order, cause you'll either get a throaty groan of pleasure or a face full of sand, so be sure to keep your sunglasses on and your mouth closed. Aalll riiight, then! Happy slatherin'

Canadian What?!

Hey guys, it's your old buddy Buster, keeping an eye on the world for you so you don't have to pay attention. You probably didn't even notice that next week is Canada Day, but that's what I'm here for, to stay ever vigilant for the chowder-headed single guys who don't pay attention to anything unless it looks good in a bikini or can improve their outlook on life after two or three glasses of it. If you're in the unfortunate position of having to explain to a woman where you are most of the time, now's the time to start dropping hints to her that Canada Day is coming up, and she'll figure you're pulling her leg again and check the calendar and be shocked that you're not lyin' for once. Tell her it's a guy thing your buddy from Toronto came up with, kinda like the Super Bowl— every year you and your homies get together, drink Canadian whisky, eat Canadian bacon, and watch hockey bloopers and the all-Canada lumberjack championships and Mike Myers movies, all of which will gross her out, and she'll want no part of it. Get your story straight with all your buddies, find somebody to agree to be from Toronto to cover your tracks, and you've got another annual event where you've got an all-day alibi, *ay?*

Housekeeping
★ ★ ★ ★

Who Needs a Dishwasher?

You can get a ton of dishes at a yard sale for a buck. They're better than paper plates, but you can still use them once or twice and toss them.

Getting By
★ ★ ★ ★

Reception Crashing as an Art Form

Have a junk car battery gift-wrapped professionally, find out the couple's names, and you'll be sleeping off a connoisseur's buzz by the time they figure it out. *(Extra: Tell foreigners it's an American custom for guests to take home a box of food.)*

Hound-Dogging
☆ ☆ ☆ ☆

Pillows, and the Women Who Love Them

Logic Need Not Apply: Dumb as it seems, it is a law of nature that a woman needs sixteen pillows on her bed. Don't ask, joke, or make snide comments when you're that close.

Vegetarian Hunting

Today I've got a tip for my fellow sporting types who like to expand their horizons by experiencing as wide a variety of women as possible. For the average burger-gobbling omni-vore like me, the elusive pale-cheeked vegetarian is a real challenge, since I'll eat anything that's not actually begging me not to. As you've probably figured out on your own, the beansprout and tofu types don't want to talk to you, let alone suck face with you after you've committed atrocities on a chicken carcass. So do what I do: When you meet a new woman, assume from the git-go that she's a vegetarian and don't blow your cover by taking her to a rib joint. Ask first what she likes to eat, and if she's a fetching veggie lass, tell her you're SO relieved because you're disgusted by flesh-eaters, too, and the mere thought of eating a fellow passenger on spaceship earth makes you nauseous. Choke down a few garden burgers with her, and she'll think you're so dad-gum enlightened and sensitive that she'll break her own rule about not putting flesh in her mouth, if you know what I mean. And afterward, of course, you can go off and celebrate with a big plate of baby-backs.

TRENDY BEVERAGES

Hey guys, it's your old pal Buster, and today I've got a tip about staying trendy without it costing you an arm and a leg. Ten years ago I figured the only time you might hear me say, "Give me that three-dollar bottle of water," would be if I was bad dehydrated and a couple of minutes away from certain death. But now, people do it all the time. And at the beach and in workout joints, you gotta have a bottle of something with a French name on it or people figure you're a hillbilly. Well, the day I start buying French water at three-dollars a pop is the day I start carryin' a Gucci purse and wearin' eyeliner and callin' my buddies Sweetheart. It ain't likely. So go ahead and invest in a bottle of the stuff, but just keep filling it with good old American tap water until it starts looking used and it's time to get another one. And by the way, the liquor store is just full of clear stuff that looks exactly like water, so use your imagination. Okay, one more: A bottle of orange juice looks exactly like orange juice if some of that clear stuff is mixed in, too.

The Single Guy Fraternity

You're a member in good standing if you think . . .

. . . a long-term relationship is five years or 50,000 miles.

. . . a walk down the aisle means you're looking for the beer section.

. . . "Till death do you part" is one of the rules of the Ultimate Fighting Championships.

. . . a double-ring ceremony is when the bartender hits the tip bell twice.

. . . monogamy is some kind of wood.

. . . the only way you'll be a groom is if it means brushing horses.

Housekeeping
★ ★ ★ ★
SOS to Anal Man

When your CD and tape collection gets so out of control it bothers even you, invite Anal Man over to watch a game and ask him to help you look for a certain CD. By the end of the game he'll have your collection stacked, dusted, and cross-referenced by artist and title.

Hound-Dogging
★ ★ ★ ★
Answering Machine Ambush

Keep the volume control of your answering machine turned completely OFF. A 2 a.m. call from a horny waitress can ruin an evening of magic.

Hound-Dogging
★ ★ ★ ★

Wedding Bliss

When the women at the wedding start crying, yank out a couple of nostril hairs, sniff loudly, and let everybody see the tears. You'll have them fighting for the chance to get in some honeymoon practice with Mr. Sensitive.

Getting By
★ ★ ★ ★

Self-Defense: The Men's Store

To keep pushy salesmen at bay, load up on bean burritos and when Mr. Fashion starts hovering too close, just blast him to the shoe department.

MIXED BABYSITTING

Man, I've got a good one for you today, guys. Here's the best way I know to survive getting stuck babysitting a nephew or something. My sister uses that Useless Guilty Uncle ploy to dump a five-year-old on me every once in awhile, and it works pretty good because, well, I'm pretty much a Useless Guilty Uncle so sometimes I have to step up and be responsible. But here's something all parents know and most bachelors don't: Two kids are easier than one, honest to God! So as soon as I know there's no way I can get out of it, I call this friend of mine who's got a whole house full of kids, and I ask him if I can borrow one that's my nephew's age. Usually he'll say sure, and tell me I can keep the kid 'til he's in high school if I want to. Then I call a girlfriend and sound all excited, you know, "Kids are such a hoot! Wanta come over and have some fun with us?!" and women think that's just the sweetest thing and usually fall for it. But the best thing is that when you've got two kids, they don't want to have anything to do with the grown-ups and they'll disappear for hours at a time while you and your girl do some adult catching up.

Reading at the Coffee House

Man oh man, guys, today I've got a simple trolling tip that works great on women that go to these new coffee house/reading room joints that're so trendy right now—I'm three for four and I've only been doing it a month. Just be sure to take advantage before the next big thing puts these joints out of business, it's bound to happen. Check out some yard sales or go to a thrift shop and buy a humongous book that you could prop up the couch with—something you'd never read, but it oughta have "Civilization" in the title, or maybe "Literature" or "Psychology"or some brain-wrecking thing like that. You don't have to know anything about it as long as you can say, "I find the subject fascinating and devour everything I can find." That word "devour" makes women squirm, and they don't even know why. Then immediately change the subject and stay as far away from the topic of your book as possible, and ask her what *she* likes to read, and if you can pretend to look absolutely mesmerized while she blathers on about her latest chick book, then the next thing you know, you'll be sharing the morning paper.

Hound-Dogging
☆ ☆ ☆ ☆

The "So-Pathetic-It's-Cute" Ploy

When you screw up big time, buy a peace offering and wrap it with three different kinds of wrapping paper, duct tape, and grass rope. A Band-Aid on your finger and a blood smear on the package can add a dramatic touch.

Housekeeping
★ ★ ★ ★

Helping the Homeless Help You

After your next party, give a homeless guy some trash bags and turn him loose. You get your place cleaned for free and do your bit for humanity and the environment with one easy move.

Getting By
★ ★ ★ ★

Instant Breakfast

Before you crash at night, chop up one of those frozen breakfast deals and put it in a big mug in the fridge. In the morning, nuke it while you shower and "drink" it right out of the mug on your way to work.

Getting By
★ ★ ★ ★

Grill Cheese with Iron

Slap some cheese between two slices of bread, wrap it in tinfoil, iron that sucker, and *voila*: a quick meal with zero clean-up.

SCHOOLTEACHER SEASON

Hidee ho, everybody, it's your good buddy Buster, and today I've got a great tip for you guys who like to sample a varied menu of female companionship, but have looked for love in all the wrong places so many times you just can't fool any of the locals any of the time anymore. Well, guess what? School is back in, and you know what that means—school *teachers* are back in, many of them fresh out of teacher's college full of high hopes and heaving hormones, and if you've got a buddy who's a coach or something, they can usually tell you which ones are available and where you might find them after work. Believe me, after they've battled a roomful of screeching snot-nosed brats all day, they need something to melt away the tension, like a good book and soft music, or what I always recommend, three shots of chilled tequila and a backrub— it makes learning fun, believe me.

PTAS FOR BABES

Whoo boy! What a reaction! You might remember me telling you last time that fresh young schoolteachers are an important resource that many bachelors overlook, probably because we still think they're going to make us do something we hate. Well, you wouldn't BELIEVE the emails I got after that one, and the most Frequently Asked Question by far was, Okay, but how do you meet 'em? Easy: Where do all grownups meet teachers? PTA meetings, duh! Now you're sayin', Hey, I'm a bachelor, not a breeder, I don't have kids. Even better! Because you have suddenly taken a keen interest in the academic development of your knot-headed nephew, or the kid next door, or whoever happens to have an edible-looking educator. That makes you even more attractive to them, you see, because it's not even your own rug-rat you're interested in, so she'll think you're a sensitive, caring man who gives of himself. Kabing, kabong. Ducks in a barrel, guys, ducks in a barrel.

Housekeeping
★ ★ ★ ★
Towel Hygiene

You can dry off with the same towel pretty much indefinitely, but if you pick it up and it doesn't change shape, it's time to head to the laundromat.

Housekeeping
★ ★ ★ ★
The Pristine Boudoir

Keep a car cover over your bed, sleep on top of it, and cover it up with a couple of army blankets. Whip it off to dazzle your next guest with your clean linen.

The Single Guy Fraternity

You're a member in good standing
if you think . . .

. . . it's no accident that the words "commitment" and
"institution" both apply to mental hospitals
and marriage.
. . . finding a soul mate means matching up shoes.
. . . a "prenuptual agreement" is deciding on the
safest place to meet after she's married.
. . . a "steady girl" is one that doesn't wobble much
when she's drinking.
. . . "mating for life" means scoring quick so you
won't die from not getting any.

Getting By
★ ★ ★ ★

Gourmet Leftovers

Cut a flap into an old suitcase, and you can harvest enough goodies off of room-service trays in the halls of a fancy hotel to eat like a king for a week.

Hound-Dogging
☆ ☆ ☆ ☆

Escaping the Dry Snuggle

    If it turns out that she actually just wants to "snuggle by the fire" and not toast your bare buns, poke a burning log to get some sparks going, reel back screaming and clawing at your eyes, and with any luck you'll get away in time to grab a beer with the guys.